Let the Warfare Begin

Militant Warfare Prayers for Healing, Deliverance, Breaking of Curses, and Breakthroughs

For we are not wrestling with flesh and blood [contending only with physical opponents], but against the despotisms, against the powers, against [the master spirits who are] the world rulers of this present darkness, against the spirit forces of wickedness in the heavenly (supernatural) sphere
—Ephesians 6:12

See, I have this day appointed you to the oversight of the nations and of the kingdoms to root out and pull down, to destroy and to overthrow, to build and to plant.
—Jeremiah 1:10

By Robin Dinnanauth
Author of *Miracles Still Happen*

Xulon PRESS

To: Sister India
Shalom & Blessings
Robin Dmanelle
Eph 6:12

Contents

About the Author

Robin Dinnanauth is an active evangelist ministering the gospel of the Lord Jesus Christ and demonstrating God's healing and delivering power both in the United States and around the world. He has been used mightily by God in healing and deliverance, preaching in crusades and revival meetings. He is out in the front, battling Satan and leading the charge against demonic forces that appear to have so many souls in torment. He is also the author of the best-selling books *Miracles Still Happen* and *Every Day with Jesus*.

As a highly sought-after crusader and revival speaker whom God has raised up as a prophetic voice to the world, Robin is calling people to Jesus Christ through the good news of the gospel and the power of the blood of the Lamb. Thousands experience the saving, healing, and delivering message of Jesus Christ as Robin ministers hope to the sick, the afflicted, and the hurting.

He is known for his dynamic and anointed prayer and his healing and deliverance ministry. An ordained minister, pastor, overseer, and sought-after conference speaker, he is also the founder of Emmanuel Full Gospel Assemblies of Churches, Robin Healing Ministries, and Emmanuel Bible Training Institute.

Acknowledgments

With a grateful heart, I would like to thank some very special people who have made a great impact in my life and also helped me with this project:

My beautiful wife, Veronica, and our wonderful children, Justin and Josiah, who always stood by my side and supported me in all my projects.

Barry Adams of Father Heart Communications, who granted me permission to use the "Father's Love Letter."

Minister Gene B. Moody of Jefferson Highway Deliverance Ministries for allowing me to use quotes, prayers, and articles from his deliverance manual.

Director Al Williams and all the Robin Healing Ministries staff, who stood by my side in good times and bad times, and also for their hard work towards this project.

All the members and friends of Emmanuel Full Gospel Assemblies who have supported us in one way or another, especially the intercessory prayer group members, who have shared their ideas and also prayed for this project after so many battles.

My personal Lord and Savior Jesus Christ, who is the head of my life and has made all provision for this project. All glory and praise belong to Him.

Introduction

Power and Authority in Jesus Christ Use It or Lose It!

You [Cyrus of Persia, soon to conquer Babylon] are My battle-ax or maul and weapon of war—for with you I break nations in pieces, with you I destroy kingdoms.
—Jeremiah 51:20 AMP

I have given you authority to trample on snakes and scorpions and to overcome all the power of the enemy; nothing will harm you.
—Luke 10:19 NIV

Who are you? "You . . . are my battle-ax . . . and weapon of war—for with you I will break the nation in pieces, with you I will destroy kingdoms" (Jer. 51:20 AMP).

The Scriptures declare that the Father is counting on the believer to subdue Satan's empire. Psalm 149:5–9 says: "Let the saints be joyful in the glory and beauty [which God confers upon them]; let them sing for joy upon their beds. Let the high praises of God be in their throats and a two-edged sword in their hands, To wreak vengeance upon the nations and chastisement upon the peoples, To bind their kings with chains, and their nobles with fetters of iron, To execute upon them the judgment written. He [the Lord] is the honor of all His saints. Praise the Lord! (Hallelujah!)

Luke 4:18–19 says, "The Spirit of the Lord [is] upon Me, because He has anointed Me [the Anointed One, the Messiah] to preach the good news (the Gospel) to the poor; He has sent Me to announce release to the captives and recovery of sight to the blind, to send forth as delivered those who are oppressed [who are downtrodden, bruised, crushed, and broken down by calamity], To proclaim the accepted and acceptable year of the Lord [the day when salvation and the free favors of God profusely abound]."

Ephesians 2:10 says, "For we are God's [own] handiwork (His workmanship), recreated in Christ Jesus, [born anew] that we may do those good works which God predestined (planned beforehand) for us [taking paths which He prepared ahead of time], that we should walk in them [living the good life which He prearranged and made ready for us to live].

The Scriptures are clear that the believer has the authority over Satan and all his evil spirits, though they are admittedly the creation of the Father. Isaiah 45:7 says, "I form the light and create darkness; I make peace and create calamity; I, the LORD, do all these things." The Bible verifies that we have total authority vested in us by the Father through Jesus Christ, His only Son.

The believer is in authority over the work of God's hands. Genesis 1:28 says, "Then God blessed them, and

God said to them, 'Be fruitful and multiply; fill the earth and subdue it; have dominion over the fish of the sea, over the birds of the air, and over every living thing that moves on the earth.' "

Militant Spiritual Warfare

For we are not wrestling with flesh and blood [contending only with physical opponents], but against the despotisms, against the powers, against [the master spirits who are] the world rulers of this present darkness, against the spirit forces of wickedness in the heavenly (supernatural) sphere.
—Ephesians 6:12

Who Am I?

I am a soldier in the army of the Lord Jesus Christ, my commander-in-chief.

"Fight the good fight of the faith. Take hold of the eternal life to which you were called when you made your good confession in the presence of many witnesses" (1 Tim. 6:12). If we are warriors for Christ, then how do we fight the war? We can fight this war by spiritual warfare. The Apostle Paul shows us that Christ was a warrior for God and we are to be warriors for Christ. The war consists of two fronts: an earthly and a heavenly.

On Earth

On earth we do not war against humans, but against the demons in humans. We do not fight (physically, mentally, or

15

materially) with our brothers or sisters, saved or unsaved. We do pray for those who are unsaved to receive salvation but do not cast out their demons. For the saved, we bind up the demons and cast them out of their bodies.

We pray for salvation, deliverance, baptism, healing, and prosperity. We teach, counsel, pray, and minister as the Holy Spirit leads. In other words, we minister to all the needs of our brethren in every area of their lives. God has made provisions for every need we have in every area of our lives!

On earth we battle for our minds, which is the main battle for the human race. Physically, we fight for our bodies to be healthy. For our finances, we battle against the forces of evil by giving tithes and offerings to support the true works of God. Time is spent in following Christ daily through fellowshiping with other Christians, reading the Bible, fasting, praying, meditating, studying the Word of God, etc. We battle mentally, physically, materially, and spiritually with our time, talents, and resources.

In the Heavenlies

In the heavenlies, we war against Satan and his army of fallen angels, demons, and imps. This is mainly a spiritual battle of prayer against principalities, powers, rulers of darkness of this world, and spiritual wickedness in high places. There are two heavenlies: godly and ungodly. We ask God to loose His forces to battle for us, and we bind the forces of Satan. The Bible says, "For our struggle is not against flesh and blood, but against the rulers, against the authorities, against the powers of this dark world, and against the spiritual forces of evil in the heavenly realms" (Eph. 6:12).

Daily Vitamins

This Book of the Law shall not depart out of your mouth, but you shall meditate on it day and night, that you may observe and do according to all that is written in it. For then you shall make your way prosperous, and then you shall deal wisely and have good success.

—Joshua 1:8

The Scriptures listed below are your daily vitamins, and reading the Word of God is very important. Praying and reading the Word of God go hand in hand. *Remember to take vitamins A–Z daily.*

Anxious—Take Vitamin A
"All things work together for good for those
who love God,
who are called according to His purpose" (Rom. 8:28).

Blue—Take Vitamin B
"Bless the Lord, O my soul, and all that is
within me, bless His Holy name" (Ps. 103:1).

Crushed—Take Vitamin C
"Cast all your care on Him, because He cares for you"
(1 Pet. 5:7).

Depressed—Take Vitamin D
"Draw near to God, and He will draw near to you"
(James 4:8).

Empty—Take Vitamin E
"Enter His gates with thanksgiving, and His courts with praise. Give thanks to Him, bless His name" (Ps. 100:4).

Fearful—Take Vitamin F
"Fear not, for I am with you, do not be afraid,
for I am your God" (Isa. 41:10).

Greedy—Take Vitamin G
"Give, and it will be given to you.
A good measure, pressed down,
shaken together, running over,
will be put into your lap; for the
measure you give will be the measure you get back"
(Luke 6:38).

Hesitant—Take Vitamin H
"How beautiful upon the mountains are the feet of the messenger who announces peace, who brings good news, who announces salvation, who says to Zion, 'Your God reigns' " (Isa. 52:7).

Insecure—Take Vitamin I
"I can do all things through Christ who strengthens me"
(Phil. 4:13).

Jittery—Take Vitamin J
"Jesus Christ is the same yesterday and today and forever" (Heb. 13:8).

Know Nothing—Take Vitamin K
"Know this that the LORD is God; it is He that made us and not we ourselves" (Ps. 100:3).

Lonely—Take Vitamin L
"Lo, I am with you always, even to the end of the age" (Matt. 28:20).

Mortgaged—Take Vitamin M
"My grace is sufficient for you, for My strength is made perfect in weakness" (2 Cor. 12:9).

Nervous—Take Vitamin N
"Never, no never will I leave you or forsake you" (Heb. 13:5).

Overwhelmed—Take Vitamin O
"Overcome evil with good" (Rom. 12:21).

Perplexed or Puzzled—Take Vitamin P
"Peace I leave with you;
My peace I give to you; not as the world gives do I give to you. Let not your heart be troubled; neither let it be afraid" (John 14:27).

Quitting—Take Vitamin Q
"Watch, stand fast in the faith, be brave, be strong" (1 Cor. 16:13).

Restless—Take Vitamin R
"Rest in the Lord, and wait patiently for Him" (Ps. 37:7).

Scared—Take Vitamin S
"Stay with me, and do not be afraid;
for the one who seeks my
life seeks your life; you will be safe with me"
(1 Sam. 22:23).

Tired—Take Vitamin T
"Those who wait on the LORD shall renew their strength,
they shall mount up with wings like eagles, they shall
run and not be weary, they shall walk and not faint"
(Isa. 40:31).

Uncertain—Take Vitamin U
"Understand that I am (the LORD). Before Me no God was
formed, nor shall there be any after Me" (Isa. 43:10).

Vain—Take Vitamin V
"Vexed with unclean spirits: and they were healed
every one" (Acts 5:16).

Wondering What to Do—Take Vitamin W
"What does the LORD require of you
but to do justly, and to love
mercy, and to walk humbly with your God?"
(Mic. 6:8).

Exhausted—Take Vitamin X
"Exercise thyself rather unto godliness" (1 Tim.4:7).

Yearning for Hope—Take Vitamin Y
"Yea, though I walk through the valley
of the shadow of death,
I will fear no evil; for You are with me;
Your rod and Your staff,
they comfort me" (Ps. 23:4).

Zapped—Take Vitamin Z
"Zealous for good deeds" (Titus 2:14).

It Is Written

But He replied, It has been written, Man shall not live and be upheld and sustained by bread alone, but by every word that comes forth from the mouth of God.

— Matthew 4:4 AMP

Genesis 1:28
"God blessed them and said to them, 'Be fruitful and increase in number; fill the earth and subdue it. Rule over the fish of the sea and the birds of the air and over every living creature that moves on the ground.' "

Genesis 3:15
"And I will put enmity between you and the woman, and between your offspring and hers; he will crush your head, and you will strike his heel."

Exodus 15:3
"The LORD is a warrior; the LORD is his name."

Psalm 5:10
"Declare them guilty, O God! Let their intrigues be their downfall. Banish them for their many sins, for they have rebelled against you."

Psalm 6:10

"All my enemies will be ashamed and dismayed; they will turn back in sudden disgrace."

Psalm 7:15

"He who digs a hole and scoops it out falls into the pit he has made."

Psalm 8:6

"You made him ruler over the works of your hands; you put everything under his feet."

Psalm 10:15

"Break the arm of the wicked and evil man; call him to account for his wickedness that would not be found out."

Psalm 17:13

"Rise up, O LORD, confront them, bring them down; rescue me from the wicked by your sword.

Psalm 24:8

"Who is this King of glory? The LORD strong and mighty, the LORD mighty in battle."

Psalm 28:4

"Repay them for their deeds and for their evil work; repay them for what their hands have done and bring back upon them what they deserve."

Psalm 35:8

"May ruin overtake them by surprise—may the net they hid entangle them, may they fall into the pit, to their ruin."

Psalm 37:14
"The wicked draw the sword and bend the bow to bring down the poor and needy, to slay those whose ways are upright."

Psalm 55:9
"Confuse the wicked, O Lord; confound their speech, for I see violence and strife in the city."

Psalm 57:6
"They spread a net for my feet—I was bowed down in distress. They dug a pit in my path—but they have fallen into it themselves. Selah."

Psalm 58:6
"Break the teeth in their mouths, O God; tear out, O LORD, the fangs of the lions!"

Psalm 59:11
"But do not kill them, O Lord our shield, or my people will forget. In your might make them wander about, and bring them down."

Psalm 68:18
"When you ascended on high, you led captives in your train; you received gifts from men, even from the rebellious—that you, O LORD God, might dwell there."

Psalm 69:22
"May the table set before them become a snare; may it become retribution and a trap."

Psalm 83:9
"Do to them as you did to Midian, as you did to Sisera and Jabin at the river Kishon."

Psalm 109:17
"He loved to pronounce a curse—may it come on him; he found no pleasure in blessing—may it be far from him."

Psalm 109:28
"They may curse, but you will bless; when they attack they will be put to shame, but your servant will rejoice."

Psalm 109:29
"My accusers will be clothed with disgrace and wrapped in shame as in a cloak."

Psalm 140:9
"Let the heads of those who surround me be covered with the trouble their lips have caused."

Psalm 149:6–9
"May the praise of God be in their mouths and a double-edged sword in their hands, to inflict vengeance on the nations and punishment on the people, to bind their kings with fetters, their nobles with shackles of iron, to carry out the sentence written against them. This is the glory of all his saints. Praise the LORD."

Proverbs 26:2
"Like a fluttering sparrow or a darting swallow, an undeserved curse does not come to rest."

Isaiah 53:12
"Therefore I will give him a portion among the great, and he will divide the spoils with the strong, because he poured out his life unto death, and was numbered with the transgressors. For he bore the sin of many, and made intercession for the transgressors."

Isaiah 54:17
"No weapon forged against you will prevail, and you will refute every tongue that accuses you. This is the heritage of the servants of the LORD, and this is their vindication from me," declares the LORD.

Jeremiah 1:10
"See, today I appoint you over nations and kingdoms to uproot and tear down, to destroy and overthrow, to build and to plant."

Jeremiah 48:10
"A curse on him who is lax in doing the LORD 's work! A curse on him who keeps his sword from bloodshed!"

Jeremiah 51:20
"You are my war club, my weapon for battle—with you I shatter nations, with you I destroy kingdoms."

Matthew 5:44
"But I tell you: Love your enemies and pray for those who persecute you."

Matthew 10:7–8
"As you go, preach this message: 'The kingdom of heaven is near.' Heal the sick, raise the dead, cleanse those who

have leprosy, drive out demons. Freely you have received, freely give."

Matthew 12:29
"Or again, how can anyone enter a strong man's house and carry off his possessions unless he first ties up the strong man? Then he can rob his house."

Matthew 18:18
"I tell you the truth, whatever you bind on earth will be bound in heaven, and whatever you loose on earth will be loosed in heaven."

Matthew 28:20
"And teaching them to obey everything I have commanded you. And surely I am with you always, to the very end of the age."

Luke 4:18
"The Spirit of the Lord is on me, because he has anointed me to preach good news to the poor. He has sent me to proclaim freedom for the prisoners and recovery of sight for the blind, to release the oppressed."

Luke 8:1
"After this, Jesus traveled about from one town and village to another, proclaiming the good news of the kingdom of God. The Twelve were with him."

Luke 10:18
"He replied, 'I saw Satan fall like lightning from heaven.' "

Luke 10:19

"I have given you authority to trample on snakes and scorpions and to overcome all the power of the enemy; nothing will harm you."

Luke 11:22

"But when someone stronger attacks and overpowers him, he takes away the armor in which the man trusted and divides up the spoils."

John 12:31

"Now is the time for judgment on this world; now the prince of this world will be driven out."

John 16:11

"And in regard to judgment, because the prince of this world now stands condemned."

John 16:20

"I tell you the truth; you will weep and mourn while the world rejoices. You will grieve, but your grief will turn to joy."

Romans 16:20

"The God of peace will soon crush Satan under your feet. The grace of our Lord Jesus be with you."

1 Corinthians 4:12

"We work hard with our own hands. When we are cursed, we bless; when we are persecuted, we endure it."

2 Corinthians 10:4

"The weapons we fight with are not the weapons of the world. On the contrary, they have divine power to demolish strongholds."

Ephesians 3:10

"His intent was that now, through the church, the manifold wisdom of God should be made known to the rulers and authorities in the heavenly realms."

Ephesians 6:12

"For our struggle is not against flesh and blood, but against the rulers, against the authorities, against the powers of this dark world and against the spiritual forces of evil in the heavenly realms."

Ephesians 6:16

"In addition to all this, take up the shield of faith, with which you can extinguish all the flaming arrows of the evil one."

Colossians 2:15

"And having disarmed the powers and authorities, he made a public spectacle of them, triumphing over them by the cross."

2 Timothy 1:10

"But it has now been revealed through the appearing of our Savior, Christ Jesus, who has destroyed death and has brought life and immortality to light through the gospel."

2 Timothy 2:26
"And that they will come to their senses and escape from the trap of the devil, who has taken them captive to do his will."

Hebrews 2:8
"And put everything under his feet. In putting everything under him, God left nothing that is not subject to him. Yet at present we do not see everything subject to him."

Hebrews 2:14
"Since the children have flesh and blood, he too shared in their humanity so that by his death he might destroy him who holds the power of death—that is, the devil."

James 4:7
"Submit yourselves, then, to God. Resist the devil, and he will flee from you."

1 John 3:8
"He who does what is sinful is of the devil, because the devil has been sinning from the beginning. The reason the Son of God appeared was to destroy the devil's work."

1 John 5:5
"Who is it that overcomes the world? Only he who believes that Jesus is the Son of God."

Revelation 12:11
"They overcame him by the blood of the Lamb and by the word of their testimony; they did not love their lives so much as to shrink from death."

Revelation 12:17

"Then the dragon was enraged at the woman and went off to make war against the rest of her offspring—those who obey God's commandments and hold to the testimony of Jesus."

How to Pray

I desire therefore that in every place men should pray, without anger or quarreling or resentment or doubt [in their minds], lifting up holy hands.

— 1 Timothy 2:8

Teach Me to Pray

Many people ask me, "Pastor Robin, can you teach me how to pray?" Well, I am willing to teach anyone how to pray; but my way may not work for you, and the way I learn to pray from a book may not work for you either. The best way to learn to pray is the way Jesus taught His disciples. Jesus taught His disciples how to pray, and we can follow this pattern through the Scriptures below. This is the best way to do it.

A Close Look at the Model Prayer

When the disciples came to Jesus, they said, "Teach us to pray," not "Teach us a prayer." Jesus responded to their request by using a method commonly employed by the Jewish rabbi. The rabbi often listed certain topics of truth and then under each point provided a complete outline. In this model prayer, Jesus used this same teaching pattern.

He gave topics and instructed, "After this manner, therefore, pray."

Our Father

The words *Our Father* indicate nearness, but the words *in heaven* imply distance. Psalm 139 reveals, however, that God is everywhere. When we pray to our Father in heaven, it does not emphasize the distance between us and the Father, but it immediately brings us from the natural world to a powerful spiritual plane. It assures us that God has at His disposal the entire resources of the supernatural realm with which to respond to the requests presented in the remainder of the model prayer. When we pray "our Father in heaven," we are immediately linked through Christ with a supernatural God with unlimited supernatural resources that can be used in prayer.

Hallowed Be Your Name

When we become members of God's family, our heavenly Father's name is given to us, just as a child who is adopted in the natural world assumes the name of his new dad. Our spiritual adoption gives us the right to call God "Father" and receive all the benefits associated with His name, because we are now heirs of our Father's kingdom. God's name is not just an identification label, but it is an expression of His nature and identity. When we say "hallowed be Your name," we proclaim the person, power, and authority of God. The following list identifies the seven compound names of God and their meanings:

Name	Meaning	Reference
Jehovah-Tsidkenu	Jehovah Our Righteousness	Jeremiah 23:6
Jehovah-M'kaddesh	Jehovah Who Sanctifies	Exodus 31:13
Jehovah-Shalom	Jehovah Is Peace	Judges 6:24
Jehovah-Shammah	Jehovah Is There	Ezekiel 48:35
Jehovah-Rophe	Jehovah Heals	Exodus 15:26
Jehovah-Jireh	Jehovah My Provider	Genesis 22:14
Jehovah-Nissi	Jehovah My Banner	Exodus 17:15
Jehovah-Rohi	Jehovah My Shepherd	Psalm 23:1

When we pray for others, we can use these names to intercede for God to work in their lives. Here is an example: "I pray for my wife, that You will be Jehovah-Shalom to her. I pray that You will be her Jehovah-Jireh, providing her every need this day. Jehovah-Nissi, I pray that Your banner will reign over her life. I pray that as Jehovah-M'kaddesh, You will sanctify her this day."

Your Kingdom Come

In Greek, Hebrew, and Aramaic, the term *kingdom of God* refers to the kingship, sovereignty, reign, or ruling activity of God. It is the expression of God's nature in action. God's realm of operation can be viewed in terms of its inclusive universal organization as the kingdom of God; its local visible organization as the church through which the kingdom is extended; and individuals of which the kingdom is composed, that is, all true believers born into this kingdom.

Sometime in the future, the kingdom of God will be established in visible form. We do not know the exact timing of this (Acts 1:7), but according to the Word of God, it is certain. All the kingdoms of the world will become the property of God, the evil kingdom of Satan will be defeated, and our King will reign forever (Rev. 11:15).

The centrality of the kingdom message is clear in the New Testament record. It is mentioned several times in Matthew, 16 times in Mark, and 38 times in Luke. Jesus began His earthly ministry by declaring the arrival of the kingdom (Matt.4:17). He ended His earthly ministry by speaking of things pertaining to the kingdom (Acts 1:3). In between the beginning and ending of His earthly ministry, the emphasis was always on the kingdom. He was constantly declaring He must preach its message in other places (Luke 4:43). Every parable of Jesus related to the kingdom, and His life patterned its principles.

Jesus indicated that we, as believers, were to give similar emphasis to the kingdom: "But seek first the kingdom of God and His righteousness, and all these things shall be added to you" (Matt. 6:33). This verse indicates where we should focus our praying, preaching, teaching, and living. It should all be targeted on the kingdom of God. If we seek first the kingdom, it assures the answer to the other petitions that follow in the model prayer.

Praying "Your kingdom come" is more than a prayer for the return of Jesus and establishing of the kingdom in its final form. When we pray "Your kingdom come," we are actually declaring that our Father will reign in the lives of believers, unbelievers, and the entire earth. We are interceding that God will be acknowledged as King and that life here on earth will be regulated by His commands. When we say "Your kingdom come," we are actually asking God to remove anything that is in rebellion against His kingdom, including words, attitudes, desires, behavior, etc., in ourselves and others.

Your Will Be Done on Earth as It Is in Heaven
In general, the Bible refers to the will of God in three different senses.

1. In some passages, *the will of God* is another way of saying "the law of God" (Ps. 48:8).
2. *The will of God* is also used to designate anything that God expressly desires; this may properly be called God's "perfect will" (1Tim. 2:4).
3. Finally, *the will of God* may refer to what God permits or allows to happen. This may properly be called God's "permissive will."

The Bible's teaching about the will of God expresses more than mere doctrine; it intersects with our lives as believers on an everyday basis. We must learn what God's will is, and we must commit ourselves to do His will.

We are to pray that God's will and purpose be fulfilled in our lives according to His eternal plan. If this is our prayer and commitment, then we can rest assured that our present and future are in the protective care of our heavenly Father. We can determine God's will primarily through His revealed Word, the Bible, and the Holy Spirit's leading in our hearts.

Give Us This Day Our Daily Bread
In the model prayer, we seek first the kingdom when we declare "Your kingdom come" over every circumstance in our lives. We submit in righteousness to our heavenly

Father's will, declaring, "Your will be done." Now we can pray with assurance, "Give us this day our daily bread," asking that our needs be met to enable us to fulfill His will and extend His kingdom.

"Give us" acknowledges that God is our source, not a denomination or a company paycheck. The Greek word translated "daily" in this model prayer occurs nowhere else in the Bible. It means "necessary or essential bread, sufficient for our sustenance and support." Its use in this context confirms that the model prayer Jesus taught is to be prayed each day. The prayer is for "bread," which indicates both spiritual and material sustenance. The word "us" denotes that we intercede for this daily bread of provision for others as well as ourselves.

And Forgive Us Our Debts, as We Forgive Our Debtors

We must learn to both receive and give forgiveness for personal offenses and injustices caused to us by others. Personal offenses occur when we offend ourselves and God through our own sin; and we deal with it by asking Him to forgive us when we say, "Forgive us our debts."

The Bible declares, "If we say that we have no sin, we deceive ourselves, and the truth is not in us. If we confess our sins, He is faithful and just to forgive us our sins and to cleanse us from all unrighteousness" (1 John 1:8–9). When we confess our known sin, God forgives our unknown sin as well as what we have confessed, cleansing us from *all* unrighteousness.

The second area in which forgiveness must be manifested is in forgiving others of direct and indirect offenses. A direct offense occurs when we are offended by someone. Indirect offenses occur when someone hurts a friend or relative and we take up the offense. Jesus taught that we were to deal with such misdeeds by praying, "Forgive us our debts, as we forgive our debtors."

The literal rendering of this verse in Greek is "as we forgave our debtors." Thus the verse could read, "Forgive us our debts, as we have forgiven others." The idea is that before we ever seek forgiveness for our sins against God, we are to have already forgiven those who have sinned against us.

Jesus taught this principle in the parable of the unjust servant in Matthew 18:22–35. This story illustrates that God's forgiveness precedes human forgiveness. Human forgiveness is a reflection of God's forgiveness, and God's forgiveness becomes real for us only when we are willing to forgive one another. Jesus summarized these truths when He declared: "If you have anything against anyone, forgive him, that your Father in heaven may also forgive your trespasses. But if you do not forgive, neither will your Father in heaven forgive your trespasses" (Mark 11:25).

Satan causes offenses in your family, between friends, in your business relationships, and in your church. The Bible states that "offenses will come" (Matt. 18:7). How will you deal with these issues when they arise? Will you intercede about them in prayer or talk about them through gossip?

And Do Not Lead Us into Temptation, But Deliver Us from the Evil One

Jesus taught us to pray, "Do not lead us into temptation," but James indicates God does not tempt man: "Let no one say when he is tempted, 'I am tempted by God'; for God cannot be tempted by evil, nor does He Himself tempt anyone" (James 1:13). So who is the tempter to whom

Jesus is referring? The Bible clearly reveals that this is the role of our enemy, Satan (Matt. 4:3; 1 Thess. 3:5).

The Scriptures repeatedly warn of temptations that come from the devil (Matt. 4:1; 1 Cor. 7:5; 1 Thess. 3:5). The Bible explains that "each one is tempted when he is drawn away by his own desires and enticed. Then, when desire has conceived, it gives birth to sin; and sin, when it is full grown, brings forth death"(James 1:14–15).

Satan is the tempter, but we are drawn into his snare when we allow our fleshly desires to entice us. Such desires birth sin, and sin results in death. Some of Satan's attacks arise from uncontrolled evil passions from within, while other temptations come from without through our senses of hearing, seeing, feeling, touching, or tasting. Whatever their source, the apostle Paul assures us, "No temptation has overtaken you except such as is common to man; but God is faithful, who will not allow you to be tempted beyond what you are able, but with the temptation will also make the way of escape, that you may be able to bear it" (1 Cor. 10:13).

When we pray, "Do not lead us into temptation," we are asking God to preserve us from the enticement to sin. Even Jesus was not delivered from temptation but was preserved in it (Heb. 4:15). The apostle John assures us, "We know (absolutely) that any one born of God does not (deliberately and knowingly) practice committing sin, but the One Who was begotten of God carefully watches over and protects him—Christ's divine presence within him preserves him against the evil—and the wicked one does not lay hold (get a grip) on him or touch (him)" (1 John 5:18 AMP).

In Ephesians 6:10–18, the apostle Paul provides detailed information about the evil one and the spiritual armor that

God provides for our defense. Paul emphatically declares we should be strong in the Lord and in the power of His might and stand boldly in the face of these evil forces (Eph. 6:10, 11, 13). He decrees that it is possible to stand against every wile (deceit, cunning, craftiness) of the devil. Paul admonishes that we should war a good warfare (1 Tim. 1:18), fight an effective fight of faith (1 Tim. 6:12), and battle intelligently with purpose (1 Cor. 9:26).

Paul emphasizes that the battle is not a natural one and that natural weapons are ineffective. Spiritual battles must be fought with spiritual weapons.

> Therefore take up the whole armor of God, that you may be able to withstand in the evil day, and having done all to stand. Stand therefore, having girded your waist with truth, having put on the breastplate of righteousness, and having shod your feet with the preparation of the gospel of peace; above all, taking the shield of faith with which you will be able to quench all the fiery darts of the wicked one. And take the helmet of salvation, and the sword of the Spirit, which is the word of God; praying always with all prayer and supplication in the Spirit, being watchful to this end with all perseverance and supplication for all the saints.
>
> Ephesians 6:13–18

The purpose of the armor is to enable you to stand against the wiles of the enemy, Satan. Paul commands you to put on this spiritual armor, which means it is your responsibility to appropriate what God has provided. To "put on" means you take hold of something and apply it to yourself.

**For Yours Is the Kingdom and the Power
and the Glory Forever**

The word *for* indicates the authority by which the model prayer has been prayed. It means because the kingdom, power, and glory belong to God, we can claim the provisions, promises, and protection of this prayer.

When we arrive at this final portion of the model prayer and declare "Yours is the kingdom," we are coming into agreement with everything God says about His kingdom: "Do not fear, little flock, for it is your Father's good pleasure to give you the kingdom" (Luke 12:32). It is His kingdom, but as heirs, it is our kingdom also. It is a legacy conferred by our Father, and it pleases Him to give it to us.

The word for "power" is *dunamis,* from which the English words *dynamic* and *dynamite* come. When we end our prayer with "Yours is the power," we are acknowledging the dynamic power of God with its dynamite-like potential for fulfilling our petitions. When we declare "Yours is the power," God echoes back to us the words of Jesus: "I give you power over all the power of the enemy." This assures the answer to all we have interceded for in the model prayer.

We then declare, "Yours is the glory!" Glory is one of the richest words of the English language. No single word can serve as a good synonym, but here are some words that describe it: honor, praise, splendor, radiance, power, exaltation, worthiness, likeness, beauty, renown, and rank.

Jesus said, "And the glory which you gave Me, I have given them that they may be one just as We are one" (John 17:22). The same glory with which Jesus was glorified by the Father is a gift to us. All we have to do is claim it.

You should be going from glory to glory, not from defeat to defeat. You may be discouraged and despondent and feel cold and lifeless spiritually, but the Word of the Lord to you today is this: "Arise from the depression and prostration in which circumstances have kept you; rise to a new life. Shine, be radiant with the glory of the Lord; for your light is come, and the glory of the Lord is risen upon you" (Isa. 60: 1–2, AMP).

God's glory guarantees the following:

- Provision (Phil. 4:19; Eph. 3:16)
- Strength (Col. 1:11)
- Joy (Isa. 66:5; 1 Pet. 1:8; 1 Chron. 16:10)
- Liberty (Isa. 60:1)
- Rest (Isa. 11:10)
- Sanctification (Exod. 29:43)
- Unity with other believers (John 17:22)

The word *forever* means exactly what it says— "forever"; that is "eternal, having no end." As we conclude our prayer, we are ascribing the kingdom, power, and glory to our Father—*forever.* We are linking ourselves in an eternal bond with our Father because we are acknowledging that we share in His kingdom, power, and glory.

A Model Prayer

Luke 11:1–2
- Verse 1: "And it came to pass, that, as he was praying in a certain place, when he ceased, one of his disciples said unto him, 'Lord, teach us to pray, as John also taught his disciples.' "
- Verse 2: "So He said to them, 'When you pray, say, "Our Father in heaven, hallowed be Your name." ' "

How to Pray

Matthew 6:5–13

- Verse 5: "And when you pray, you shall not be like the hypocrites. For they love to pray standing in the synagogues and on the corners of the streets, that they may be seen by men. Assuredly, I say to you, they have their reward."
- Verse 6: "But you, when you pray, go into your room, and when you have shut your door, pray to your father who is in the secret place; and your Father who sees in secret will reward you openly."
- Verse 7: "And when you pray, do not use vain repetitions as the heathen do. For they think that they will be heard for their many words."
- Verse 8: "Therefore do not be like them. For your Father knows the things you have need of before you ask Him."
- Verses 9:13: "In this manner, therefore, pray:

  Our Father in heaven,
    Hallowed be Your name.
  Your kingdom come.
    Your will be done
    On earth as it is in heaven.
  Give us this day our daily bread.
  And forgive us our debts,
    As we forgive our debtors.
  And do not lead us into temptation,
    But deliver us from the evil one.
    For Yours is the kingdom and the power and the glory forever. Amen."

How to Fast

Matthew 6:16–18

- Verse 16: "Moreover, when you fast, do not be like the hypocrites, with a sad countenance, for they disfigure their faces that they may appear to men to be fasting. Assuredly, I say to you, they have their reward."
- Verse 17: "But you, when you fast, anoint your head and wash your face."
- Verse 18: "So that you do not appear to men to be fasting, but to your Father who is in the secret place; and your Father who sees in secret will reward you openly."

Help in Praying

Romans 8:26–27

- Verse 26: "Likewise the Spirit also helps in our weaknesses. For we do not know what we should pray for as we ought, but the Spirit Himself makes intercession for us with groanings which cannot be uttered."
- Verse 27: "Now He who searches the hearts knows what the mind of the Spirit is, because He makes intercession for the saints according to the will of God."

Hebrews 4:12–16

- Verse 12: "For the word of God is living and powerful, and sharper than any two-edged sword, piercing even to the division of soul and spirit, and of joints and marrow, and is a discerner of the thoughts and intents of the heart."

- Verse 13: "And there is no creature hidden from His sight, but all things are naked and open to the eyes of Him to whom we must give account."
- Verse 14: "Seeing then that we have a great High Priest who has passed through the heavens, Jesus the Son of God, let us hold fast our confession."
- Verse 15: "For we do not have a High Priest who cannot sympathize with our weaknesses, but was in all points tempted as we are, yet without sin."
- Verse 16: "Let us therefore come boldly to the throne of grace, that we may obtain mercy and find grace to help in time of need."

What Should I Do to Receive My Breakthrough?

So I say to you, Ask and keep on asking and it shall be given you; seek and keep on seeking and you shall find; knock and keep on knocking and the door shall be opened to you. For everyone who asks and keeps on asking receives; and he who seeks and keeps on seeking finds; and to him who knocks and keeps on knocking, the door shall be opened. What father among you, if his son asks for a loaf of bread, will give him a stone; or if he asks for a fish, will instead of a fish give him a serpent? Or if he asks for an egg, will give him a scorpion? If you then, evil as you are, know how to give good gifts [gifts that are to their advantage] to your children, how much more will your heavenly Father give the Holy Spirit to those who ask and continue to ask Him!
—Luke 11:9–13

Receiving healing, deliverance, and breakthrough can be very simple. Every believer has been promised this. To experience your healing, deliverance, and breakthrough, follow these six basic steps:

1. Identify your problems.
2. Forgive, pray, and get yourself right with God.
3. Break the curses and soul ties on you and your descendants.
4. Cast out the demons (using the prayers written in this book).
5. Pray for healing of your soul and body.
6. Discipline your life by changing your way of thinking and acting.

In addition, pray deliverance: break biblical curses and soul ties, renounce occult and false religions, and loose godly spirits. Destroy and remove cursed objects from your house, car, office, working area, position, etc. In some cases, if the sickness or demonic spirits do not leave, find out what the legal right is and remove it. Ask God what it is; command that sickness or demon to leave. Also, seeking agreement from another believer is recommended.

Curses

But if they confess their own and their fathers' iniquity in their treachery which they committed against Me—and also that because they walked contrary to Me I also walked contrary to them and brought them into the land of their enemies—if then their uncircumcised hearts are humbled and they then accept the punishment for their iniquity, then will I [earnestly] remember My covenant with Jacob, My covenant with Isaac, and My covenant with Abraham, and [earnestly] remember the land.

—Leviticus 26:40–42 AMP

A curse is a type of demonic tie between the living, or the living and the dead. Curses speak of oaths, binding, and placing punishment upon others. God can curse us for not following His laws. We can curse ourselves and bind ourselves under a curse. We can curse others and bind them under a curse if we have the authority to do so. We can be cursed through our ancestors from one generation to another. We can be cursed even from our mothers' wombs. We can bring curses into our houses with inanimate objects and by involvement in ungodly worship and chanting.

Inanimate cursed objects are objects that are used by different cultures to do devil worship. If you have a cursed object in your house, you are cursed. A cursed object does not just sit idle in your house. It will cause trouble for you. There are demons that live in or around the cursed object.

Do you feel an unusual attraction or repulsion to some object in your home, office, or car? You may have a demonic tie to it. I remember one day a couple came to me to pray with them because ever since they had come back from their first wedding anniversary vacation, they had started to have arguments for no reason. While I was praying, the Holy Spirit revealed to me that a gift had been given to them while they were on vacation. With the help of the Holy Spirit, they remembered a woman had given them a doll while they were on the beach. I immediately broke all curses on that inanimate object and renounced every demonic tie, in Jesus' name.

Some inanimate objects that are very demonic and that will bring curses in your houses, offices, cars, yards, etc., are as follows: images of snakes, tigers, elephants, frogs, Mother Mary, Hindu religious gods and devotees; bamboo plants; lucky charms; horseshoes over doors; chimes; signs of ohm; burning of incense; books of Harry potter; images of Buddha; seashells; etc and the list can go on and on.

In order for you to break the curse from your house, car, office, yard, business, etc., you must clean the entire environment and your body of cursed objects. If you have cursed objects in your possession, you become accursed and will have demons living with you. They don't just come to live in your house or in your body; they come to torment you and your family.

Breaking of Curses

When the curse is broken, there is a release, as if a tie has been severed. I have always wanted to see the connection in the spiritual world of the curse emanating from someone and landing on someone else. We can curse ourselves, or we can be cursed by others. How does the release occur? Is the tie suddenly severed, or does the demon suddenly leave, or what really happens? This can be done only by casting out that spirit that ties you up or breaking the curses through militant spiritual warfare prayers.

Break the curses from your life, house, job, etc. *Get them out now!* How can you break yourself free from these curses and bring total deliverance to your body and house? The answer is simple: get into militant warfare prayers and physical housecleaning.

There are five steps to cleaning your house breaking of curses and getting into militant warfare prayers:

1. Pray the seven-way prayer of forgiveness: forgive your ancestors, descendants, and others for all sins; ask God to forgive and bless them with all spiritual blessings; ask God to forgive you; forgive yourself for sins against your body; and finally ask forgiveness for worshiping other gods.
2. Break curses and soul ties from others (ancestors) and to others (descendants), and break curses of psychic, Hindu, Muslim, Buddhist or Catholic prayers.
3. Clean out your house of all objects, or exorcise objects you do not own.

4. Anoint your house and all godly objects with oil, and cast evil spirits out of the house, car, yard, office, etc.
5. Cast out demons that came in through curses from demonic objects.

Put On the Armor of

Put on God's whole armor [the armor of a heavy-armed soldier which God supplies], that you may be able successfully to stand up against [all] the strategies and the deceits of the devil.

—Ephesians 6:11

Are you ready to get into militant warfare prayers? Well, it is important to put on the armor of God so that you can stand against the works of evil. Ephesians 6:10–18 says:

In conclusion, be strong in the Lord [be empowered through your union with Him]; draw your strength from Him [that strength which His boundless might provides]. Put on God's whole armor [the armor of a heavy-armed soldier which God supplies], that you may be able successfully to stand up against [all] the strategies and the deceits of the devil. For we are not wrestling with flesh and blood [contending only with physical opponents], but against the despotisms, against the powers, against [the master spirits who are] the world rulers of this present darkness, against the spirit forces of wickedness in the heavenly (supernatural) sphere. Therefore put on God's complete armor, that you may be able to resist and stand your ground on the evil day [of danger], and, having done all [the crisis demands], to stand [firmly in your place]. Stand therefore [hold your ground], having tightened the belt of truth around your loins and having put on the breastplate of integrity and of moral rectitude and right standing with God, and having shod your feet in preparation [to face the enemy with the firm-footed stability, the promptness, and the readiness produced by the good news] of the Gospel of peace. Lift up over all the [covering] shield of saving faith, upon which you can quench all the flaming missiles of the wicked [one]. And take the helmet of salvation and the sword that the Spirit wields, which is the Word of God. Pray at all times (on every occasion, in every season) in the Spirit, with all [manner of] prayer and entreaty. To that end keep alert and watch with strong purpose and perseverance, interceding in behalf of all the saints (God's consecrated people).

Belt of Truth

"I place around my waist the belt of truth. I will know the truth and the truth will make me free. I am free because whoever the Son sets free is free indeed. I am free from (say whatever you have been set free from). I am a son (daughter) of God. The Holy Spirit guides me into all truth. He will guide me with His eye. I have the wisdom and knowledge of God. The Holy Spirit will instruct me in the way I should go."

Breastplate of Righteousness

"I put on the breastplate of righteousness. Because of the cross, Jesus has placed on me a robe of righteousness. I am the righteousness of God. I plead the blood of Jesus over myself today. Forgive me of my sins this day. Convict me, Holy Spirit, of any wrong, and search my heart of any secret sin. The righteous are as bold as a lion. I thank You for boldness to do Your will today. Help me to speak Your Word with great boldness. I am established today in Your righteousness."

The Gospel of Peace

"My feet are shod with the preparation of the gospel of peace. Help me to be prepared to give my testimony today. I thank You that You have made a covenant with me, that Your laws and Your words are written on my heart and in my mind. You said that You put Your words in my mouth. Let my life reflect the gospel of peace. Send someone across my path to share the gospel with today. Use me, Lord, to bless someone today."

Shield of Faith

"I take up the shield of faith that quenches every fiery dart of the enemy. Faith is the victory that overcomes the world. I am an overcomer in You. I can do all things through Christ who strengthens me. I thank You for my angels. I have an angel of the Lord who encamps around me. I am protected from the evil one and delivered from the evils of this present world."

Helmet of Salvation

"I place on my head the helmet of salvation, the hope of glory. I have the mind of Christ, and no weapon formed against my mind will prosper. I think on things that are good, pure, perfect, lovely, and of good report. I will take authority over my mind today. I have authority over all the power of the enemy. I choose to cast down every vain imagination that exalts itself against the knowledge of God, and I will bring them into captivity to the obedience of Christ. I belong to Jesus, and I give the Holy Spirit control of my thoughts. I submit my mind to God. I resist the devil, and he must flee."

Sword of the Spirit

"I take the sword of the Spirit, and I use it on the offense. I will not shrink back. I am a soldier for Christ. I wrestle against principalities. I thank You for the power of Your Word. It is sharper than any two-edged sword. It will not return void, but it accomplishes the task it was sent for. Your Word is true. You are not a man that You would lie. I am a doer of Your Word. Your Word is a lamp unto my feet and a light unto my path. I will hide Your Word in my heart so that I will not sin against You."

Getting Dressed for Battle

**Militant Prayer of Preparation:
Putting on God's Armor**

- "I'm (we're) strong in You, Lord, empowered through my (our) union with You. I (we) draw strength from You, that strength which Your boundless might provides. I (we) put on the whole armor, which You supply, God, that I (we) may be able to successfully stand up against all the strategies and deceits of the devil. For I (we) wrestle not with flesh and blood, but against the principalities, against the powers, against the master spirits who are the world rulers of this present darkness, against the spirit forces of wickedness in the heavenly spirit sphere.

- "Therefore, I (we) put on Your complete armor, God, that I (we) may be able to resist and stand my (our) ground. I (we) stand, and I (we) hold my (our) ground, having tightened the girdle of truth around my (our) loins, having put on the breastplate of righteousness (integrity, moral rectitude, right standing with God), and having shod my (our) feet in preparation, promptness, and readiness with the gospel of peace. I (we) lift up over all the covering shield of faith, with which I (we) can quench all the flaming missiles of the wicked one. I (we) take the helmet of salvation and the sword of the Spirit, which is the Word of God.

- "I (we) pray at all times, on every occasion, in every season, in the Spirit, with all manner of prayer and entreaty. I (we) keep alert and watch with strong purpose and perseverance, interceding on behalf of all the saints. I (we) pray that freedom of utterance may be given me (us), that I (we) may speak boldly the mystery of the gospel for which I am (we are) an ambassador. I (we) pray I (we) may declare it boldly and courageously as I (we) ought to do, *going to work*. In Jesus' name, amen!"

Militant Warfare Prayers for Believers in Christ

You can pray in the Spirit on all occasions because the Spirit will pray through you the will of God. This builds up your inner man and gives you strength for the day. You can pray for the saints according to God's Word.

LET THE WARFARE BEGIN WITH THESE MILLIANT WARFARE PRAYERS

Militant Warfare Prayer of Thanksgiving

- "I thank You that the glory of the Lord is my rear guard.
- "I will praise You today. Let the high praises of God be in my mouth and a two-edged sword in my hand. I will praise You because You are worthy of my praise. I place on myself a garment of praise for a spirit of heaviness. Put a new song in my heart, Lord. Let Your praise be continually on my lips.
- "I thank you, Lord, that You are a God of healing, provision, and restoration. You are my healer. It is the will of God for me to be healed. You took my infirmities and bore my sicknesses. You said You heal all my diseases.
- "You are my provider. Those who seek You will not lack any good thing. You will prosper me as my soul prospers. As I seek You first, You will add all things to me. All my needs are met in Jesus. You have made a covenant with me that as I tithe and give an offering, You will supply all my needs and I will reap abundantly. You are the God of restoration.
- "As I plead with You and walk pure and upright, You will rouse yourself on my behalf and restore me to my rightful place. You will restore what the cankerworm has eaten up. You restore my soul.
- "I thank you, Lord, that I walk in the fruit of your Spirit. 'It is not by might, not by power, but by your Spirit,' says the Lord. I have love, joy, peace, patience, kindness, goodness, faithfulness, gentle-

ness, and self-control. This is my personality in You.

- "I ask You for the gifts of the Spirit. Your Word says to seek the gifts. I want to edify others through these gifts. I ask You for the message of wisdom, the message of knowledge, the gift of faith, the gift of healing, miraculous powers, the gift of prophecy, discerning of spirits, speaking in different kinds of tongues, and the interpretation of tongues.
- "Help me to encourage someone today through the power of Your Holy Spirit.
- "I pray all these in Your holy name, Jesus. Your name is above every name. All things are placed under Your feet. All authority has been given unto You in heaven and in earth. In Him we live, in Him we move, and in Him we have our being. You are Lord. Amen."

Militant Warfare Prayer for Deliverance from Curses and Evil in Your Life

Since we have power over the demons through Jesus' name, they are our slaves and must obey us as we command. We have power to command the demons to attack their own works and to destroy one another, and to shake the kingdom of evil to its very foundation. Romans 6:16 says, "Know ye not, that to whom ye yield yourselves servants of sin, but ye have obeyed from the heart that form of doctrine which was delivered you." Read 2 Peter 2:19; Matthew 12:28; Luke 11:20. When you repeat the prayer below, it will break and renounce all curses from your life, and it will cast out every evil spirit from your life and environment.

"In the most powerful name of every other name, the name of *Jesus Christ, the true and living God:*

- "I break all curses and control of witchcraft as uttering a wish of evil against me; to call for mischief or injury to fall upon; to execrate, to bring evil upon or to; to blast, vex, harass, or torment with great calamities; individuals working in concert with a specific form of evil spirit activity; satanic covens of witches and warlocks; persons dabbling with witchcraft and sorcery, casting spells, potions, enchantments, and curses; wrong kinds of psychic prayers; and witchcraft control according to what is written in the Word of God in Proverbs 26:2, Psalm109, 1 John 1:9, and Galatians 3:10–15.
- "I am now closing any door I may have opened to you, Satan, through contact with witchcraft, occult, and similar activities.
- "I am closing the door against all these things I know about and all the things I don't know about.
- "I renounce you and all your demons, and I'm closing every door I may have opened. I am redeemed by the blood of Jesus Christ, in whom I put my trust.
- "Jesus Christ became a curse on the cross for me and blotted out the handwriting of ordinances against me. I claim and apply these principles.
- "I break the curse back to twenty-five generations or even to Adam and Eve. All legal holds and legal grounds I remove now, in Jesus' name.
- "I break all curses, spells, hexes, etc., sent upon me by envious enemies who seek to harm me or kill me or wreak havoc physically, emotionally, and/or spiritually.

- I bind and order any demons to come out of me and my surroundings and return to the senders, escorted by angels to destroy that seat of witchcraft. The demons are commanded to confuse and sow terror and panic in the hearts of witches and warlocks."

Militant Warfare Prayer for Deliverance from Sin

Repeat the prayer below. It will bring deliverance from sin and unrighteousness, because He is able and just to forgive you.

- "Lord Jesus Christ, I believe You died on the cross for my sins and rose again from the dead.
- "You redeemed me by Your blood. I belong to You, and I want to live for You.
- "I confess all my sins, known and unknown. I'm sorry for them all. I renounce them all.
- "Forgive me now and cleanse me with Your blood. I thank You for the blood of Jesus Christ, which cleanses me now from all sin.
- "I come to You now as my deliverer. You know my special needs, the things that bind, that torment, that defile—that evil spirit, that unclean spirit.
- "I claim the promise of your Word, 'Whosoever that calleth on the name of the Lord shall be delivered.' I call upon You now. In the name of the Lord Jesus Christ, deliver me and set me free.
- "Satan, I renounce you and all your works. I loose myself from you, in the name of Jesus, and I command you to leave me right now, in Jesus' name. Amen."

Militant Warfare Prayer for Deliverance from Ancestors' Ties and Sins

Repeat this prayer to break ancestors' ties and sins from your life or family life. This prayer will cut all ties from past generations that were involved in any ungodly activities.

- "Lord Jesus Christ, I forgive my ancestors and descendants and anyone else who has sinned against me, and I ask You to forgive and bless them with all spiritual blessings.
- "Forgive me for my many sins, and I forgive myself for sins against my body.
- "I break all curses, charms, spells, jinxes, psychic powers, hexes, vexes, and demonic ties that bind. I break all soul ties caused by witchcraft, sorcery, bewitchment, or sexual sins.
- "Lord Jesus, restore my fragmented soul, mind, will, and emotions; send Your angels to recover anything that was stolen from me.
- "Lord Jesus, stir up the demons in my subconscious mind so that they can be identified and cast out.
- "All these things I ask in the blessed name of my Lord Jesus Christ, my Lord, Master, and Savior.
- "I now take authority over Satan and all the forces of evil according to the whole Word of God and command that they obey it.
- "In the name of Jesus Christ, I ask these things. Amen."

Militant Warfare Prayer with Authority for Freedom

Repeat this prayer to set yourself free from any bondage that you are trapped in, knowingly or unknowingly. This prayer will set you free from all ties and bondages.

- "Satan, I come against all powers, principalities, and evil forces in this world and spiritual wickedness in high places.
- "I come against all demons inside or outside of my life, my house, or in anyone present; over this city, state, nation, and world; in hell or out of hell.
- "The Bible says, 'Behold, I give unto you power to tread on serpents and scorpions, and over all the power of the enemy: and nothing shall by any means hurt you.'
- "I intend to exercise that power to set myself free. Satan, I come against you by the power and blood of Jesus Christ, by the Word of God, by the name of Jesus, by the authority of the believer, in the unity of our spirits.
- "Satan, I tell you that I sit in heavenly places with Christ Jesus.
- "I am over you, your fallen angels, your demons, and all forces of evil. I command you to line up in rank and file and order, and to come out quickly.
- "I bind every power that you have and loose myself from you, in the name of Jesus Christ.
- "Lord Jesus Christ, I ask that You would send the gifts of the Holy Spirit as needed to minister to the needs of my life and to accomplish what You want done in me today.

- "I ask that You send hosts of angels, warring angels, ministering angels, the Holy Spirit, and the seven-fold Spirit of God.
- "I ask that You cut off all communications between the demons outside and the demons inside of my life.
- "I ask that You remove all demons from the air around me. I am careful to give You all the glory, honor, praise, and credit for everything that is said or done.
- "I ask all these things in the blessed name of Jesus Christ, my Lord and Master and Savior.
- "And I take authority over Satan according to the whole Word of God. For it's in Jesus' name, I pray. Amen."

Militant Warfare Prayer for Cleaning Your House Spiritually

This prayer is very important. First remove all ungodly objects from your house, and then repeat this prayer. This prayer will bring cleanliness, physically and spiritually, in your house.

"I command all demons by these names or associated with these objects to go:

- "Books and objects identified with anything related to Satan's kingdom.
- "Pictures and images and incenses that demonstrate Hinduism, Islam, or Buddhism.
- "Sinful activities of former residents who left curses; I break those curses.

- "Knocking or noisy ghosts (poltergeist) and apparitions.
- "Owl and frog images of all types.
- "Witch's mask and fetishes used by witch doctors.
- "Objects and literature that pertain to false religions or cults, the occult, and spiritism.
- "Graven images of gods.
- "Objects dedicated to demons (idols and artifacts).
- "Ouija boards or other occult paraphernalia.
- "Prayers and worship to demons that bring curses on homes; I break those curses.
- "Mexican sun gods; idols and incense; Buddhas; hand-carved objects from Africa or the Orient; anything connected with astrology, horoscopes, fortune-telling, etc; good-luck charms; cult religions, metaphysics, Christian Science, Jehovah's Witnesses, etc; rock-and-roll records and tapes.
- "Jewelry given to me by someone that has witchcraft, hex signs, or ancient geometric and mystical motifs; jewelry designed to bring good luck and act as a talisman to chase evil.
- "Indian ankh, broken- cross peace symbol, Polynesian tikis, African jujus, Italian horn, protectors from the evil eye, hand with index and little fingers pointing up, clovers, stars, wishbones, lucky coins, mystic medals, horseshoes, religious fetishes and statues.
- "Products with cryptic cursed hidden secrets, occult curses.
- "Dolls used for witchcraft and magic, puppets, cult objects, or representations of them.
- "I bind them all and set my house free in the powerful name of Jesus Christ, my deliverer."

Militant Warfare Prayer to Release Godly Spirits

As you pray this prayer, it will release godly spirits in your life and around your house. It is very important to know that only the Spirit of God can help you.

- "Lord Jesus Christ, I ask that You direct the angels to minister to my needs.
- "I loose warring angels, ministering angels, the Holy Spirit, and the sevenfold Spirit of God.
- "I loose hosts of angels, including the following godly spirits, into my house and my life:

  - "Spirit of wisdom, Spirit of the true and living God, Spirit of the Lord, right spirit.
  - "Holy Spirit, free spirit, faithful spirit, good spirit, humble spirit, excellent spirit, spirit of Elijah.
  - "Spirit of holiness, quickening spirit, patient spirit, spirit of judgment, spirit of knowledge.
  - "New spirit, poor in spirit, Spirit of Your Father, strong in spirit, spirit of truth, spirit of adoption, spirit of meekness."

Militant Warfare Prayer for Deliverance from Foul and Evil Spirits

Foul and evil spirits can torment people easily. If you are facing any form of torment from these spirits, pray this prayer for deliverance from it.

- "In the authority of Jesus Christ, I take authority over all foul and evil spirits, authorities, princes, kings, powers, world rulers, and the highest and mightiest servants of Satan.
- "I bind them to be powerless in the mighty name of Jesus Christ.
- "Father, in the authority of the Lord Jesus Christ, I pronounce the judgment written in the Scriptures upon the evil and greedy conspirators in and over these worldwide organizations.
- "As it is written, Father, I ask You to bring upon them the judgments found in Jeremiah 17:5–6, which says, 'Cursed is the man who trusts in man and makes flesh his strength, whose heart departs from the LORD. For he shall be like a shrub in the desert, and shall not see when good comes, but shall inhabit the parched places in the wilderness, in a salt land which is not inhabited.' "

Militant Warfare Prayer for Healing

God promised us healing because His Word says healing is the children's bread. Pray this prayer for your healing.

- "I bind the spirit of infirmity. I command you and all your underlings to leave my body now, in the name of Jesus Christ.
- "I break every curse of sickness, infirmity, and organ failure. I command my body to respond to the blessing of healing and health.
- "My body is the temple of the Holy Spirit.
- "I desire a clean temple for the Holy Spirit to dwell in.

- "Father, I confess to You my sins, failures, lack of faith, and weakness.
- "Help me to trust You in the things I don't know.
- "I command the spirit of confusion to leave now, in the name of Jesus Christ.
- "Lord, I ask You to grant me the blessings of long life and good health in the service of the kingdom of God.
- "The seventy years plus blessings and the abundant life Jesus came to bring are your purpose for believers.
- "I cancel the purpose and plan of the devil to kill, steal, and destroy.
- "I refuse any part of his plan and send all his curses back to the sender now, in the name of the Lord Jesus Christ.
- "In the name of Jesus Christ, I command the body-detoxification system to be healed and every spirit that is working to be destroyed or caused to fail.
- "You must leave me now. All doubt and unbelief must leave. I rebuke you now, in the name of Jesus Christ.
- "I loose the ministering spirits for the heirs of salvation to come and minister to me now, in Jesus' name.
- "Thank You, Lord Jesus, for providing me victory over hell, death, and the grave, and power over the spirits of sickness and over all the power of the devil.
- "I ask to live to accomplish all that God has purposed for my life. Let me be a positive influence for Christ each day.
- "I break the curses of sickness, infirmity, organ failure, godlessness, nests of demons, doorways

for demons, idolatry of possessions, and ungodly holidays.

- "I break the curses listed in the book of Deuteronomy, chapters 27 and 28, and in the rest of the Bible; from diseases of Egypt; from every sickness and plague in the book of law that I have the legal right to break.
- "Lord, I ask that You show me any legal rights that Satan has in my life so that I may repent and break those curses.
- "In the name of Jesus Christ, I pray. Amen!"

Daily Militant Warfare Prayer

Praying daily is very important. Ask God for His blessings for the day, and command the day to be blessed.

- "Dear heavenly and gracious Father, thank You for divine health—mental, physical, spiritual, and material—for me and my family.
- "Thank You for all blessings known and unknown, and for showering down blessings on me and my family so great that we cannot receive them.
- "Thank You for the complete restoration of our bodies.
- "Thank You for restoring everything that the devil has stolen from me and my entire family.
- "Lord, let my day be blessed in everything that I do as it is written that everything I put my hands on shall be made prosperous.
- "Bless my going out and my coming in.
- "Let Your angels of protection provide protection for me throughout the entire day. In Jesus' name, amen."

Militant Warfare Prayer Before Eating Meals

Pray this prayer before eating your meals, asking God for His sanctifying power and blessings over the food.

- "Dear heavenly and gracious Father, I thank You for this food.
- "Bless, purify, and cleanse it so that we can be fit temples for the Holy Spirit to reside in.
- "I break any curses on it and eat it with thanksgiving. For it's in Jesus' name I pray. Amen."

Militant Warfare Prayer to Destroy the Spirit of Pride

The spirit of pride can easily destroy you. It is very important to pray against the spirit of pride because the Bible says pride goes before a fall.

- "Father, I come to You in the name of Jesus Christ.
- I know pride is an abomination to You, that a haughty look, a lying tongue, hands that shed innocent blood, a heart that deviseth wicked imaginations, feet that are swift in running to mischief, a false witness that speaketh lies, and he that soweth discord among brethren are even things You doth hate and are abominations unto You.
- "Father, I renounce these and turn away from them.
- "I humble myself before You and come to You as a little child."

Militant Warfare Prayer for Healing Through Worship

Praying for physical healing is very important. God made us perfect, and He wants us to be whole.

- "Heavenly Father, we come into Your presence to love and adore You. Thank You for Your love and Your desire for union with us. We welcome all that You wish to do through this healing prayer. We open ourselves to communication with You and Jesus through the ministry of the Holy Spirit. Come, Holy Spirit, and anoint us with healing so deep it reaches back into our bloodline, with healing so wide it impacts our friends and relatives, and with healing so high it draws us into Your holiness. Holy Spirit, come with Your fire."

The Lord's Prayer

- **Our Father, Who Art in Heaven**
  "Father God, by Your grace I come to You with all that I am and all that I ever hope to be. I am Your child, born of Your love. Jesus brought me into Your presence. You alone satisfy my soul. You in me and I in You: this is the path of healing for my soul. By Your grace, I come into Your presence with simple, trusting assurance, certain of Your love for me. In Your presence, all fear and insecurity melt away, and deep hurts become healing memories. In Your presence, I am strengthened and filled with hope. Father in heaven, I breathe the breath of heaven deep inside my spirit. Your heaven flows through

73

me. May the light of Your glory be present with me throughout this day. I love You, Father."

- **Hallowed Be Thy Name**
  "Father, I choose to live this one precious life in a way that honors Your holy name. You call me to worship, and I come. O Father, let all that is within me cry holy. Let every wound of my past dissolve in the light of Your wonderful presence. Turn my weaknesses into strengths, my failures into victories, my sorrows into joy. Perfect all that concerns me as I gaze upon Your holiness."

- **Thy Kingdom Come**
  "Father, Your kingdom of love is in my heart. It is not I who lives, but Christ who lives in me. I am identified with my risen Lord Jesus, and Your kingdom is established in my spirit. In coming to know Jesus, I am discovering who I am, precious Lord. Your kingdom has come into my emotions, and they are in a healthy balance. Your kingdom has come into my mind, and it is sanctified. Your kingdom has come into my body, and I am becoming healthy. Your kingdom rules my heart, and I live a life of richness and depth. Your kingdom has come into my mouth, and I speak words that heal and liberate. Because Your kingdom rules my life, I am resilient and filled with hope in all circumstances."

- **Thy Will Be Done**
  "Father in heaven, unite my will with that of Your Son. Thank You for giving me a spirit of submission, tender and open to the Holy Spirit. In every

circumstance, I commend myself to Your grace and choose what is pleasing to You. Father, I delight to do Your will. When I lay my life before You and say, 'Thy will be done,' You receive it as an act of worship. Wonderful Lord, You have come tenderly into the deepest struggles of my life and whispered, 'Just keep your eyes on Me. Trust Me to take care of You.' You have come into my broken heart and made it a place of worship. You have drawn me to praise You when everything in my world was in ashes. You have called me to trust beyond all reason. I lay my life upon the altar of Your love and say with joy in my soul, 'Thy will be done.' Jesus, I trust in You."

- **On Earth as It Is in Heaven**
  "Father, my heart beats with Your heart. For me, to live is Christ. Thank You, Holy Spirit, for bringing my life into harmony with heaven. Thank You, Holy Spirit, for teaching me how to walk with Jesus in His resurrected life. Thank You that the attitudes of heaven are my attitudes. I think Your thoughts and walk in Your presence. I carry the light of heaven wherever I go."

- **Give Us This Day Our Daily Bread, and Forgive Us Our Debts**
  "Father, You have always taken care of me, and You always will. You give me what I need each day and prepare for my tomorrow. My faith is growing. Thank You for my daily joy that draws me to worship when sadness comes. Thank You for Your healing balm that soothes the day's aches and pains. Thank You for Your perfect love that soaks away my fear. Your

tender daily care in every area of need draws me to my knees in worship. Thank You for walking with me day by day. In our growing friendship, you have never failed me, ever. I love You, Father. I love You, Jesus, Bread of Heaven. I love You, Holy Spirit.

- "Father, thank You for Your gift of mercy in my life, Your mercy that reaches my heart because I have forgiven those who have hurt me. I confess my sins and receive forgiveness. I am free from condemnation and safely united to You. Your truth has made me free. I love You, Father."

- **As We Forgive Our Debtors**
  "Father, by the grace of the cross, I let go of bitterness, resentment, and unforgiveness. If there are hidden roots of unforgiveness, thank You for shining Your light on them. I entrust this area to You. Thank You for turning injury into compassion and hurts into intercessions. Forgiveness brings heaven to earth. I love You, Father."

- **And Lead Us Not into Temptation**
  "Thank You, Father, for keeping me on a path that leads to holiness. By Your grace, I see temptation when it comes and brush it off the path. Your love is stronger than the urge to sin. Thank You for healing any areas of my soul that might be vulnerable to temptation. Jesus, You are my shepherd and my hiding place. You guide me to safe pastures. I am responsive to the voice of the Holy Spirit, who warns me of trouble ahead. Thank You, Father. I love You."

- **But Deliver Us from Evil**

  "Father, thank You for protecting me from every evil and for bringing me a gift of peace. You have broken the chain of oppression and delivered me from depression, anger, guilt, and fear. At the name of Jesus, every knee shall bow; addictions, perversions, hopelessness, worthlessness, loneliness, and despair must bend their knees to the name of Jesus. I cast down every argument and every high thing in me that exalts itself against the knowledge of God. I bring every thought into captivity to the obedience of Christ. Thank You for giving me the power over all the power of the enemy. Nothing shall hurt me. You have given me a spirit of praise and worship, which is my strength in the face of the enemy. Thank You for Your armor, Your name, Your blood, Your Spirit. No weapon formed against me shall prosper. Thank You, Father. I love you."

- **For Thine Is the Kingdom, and the Power, and the Glory, Forever**

  "Father, every gift You have given me, every dream, every talent, every possession, every resource, and every hope for the future, I return to You with love. All is Yours. May Your name be glorified; may Your kingdom come. Take, Lord, receive all my liberty, my memory, my understanding, my entire will—all that I have and possess. You have given all to me; to You, O Lord, I return it. All is Yours. Dispose of it wholly according to Your will. Give me Your love and Your grace, for this is sufficient for me. Amen!"

Militant Warfare Daily Prayer

"Thank You, God, for all that You are and for the blessings that fill every moment of every day. 'This is the day that the Lord has made; let us rejoice and be glad in it' " (Ps. 118:24).

- "I open my spirit to You, and I give thanks for Your life that fills every cell of my body and life.
- "I open my eyes to You, and I give thanks for Your light that warms and brightens my day.
- "I open my heart to You, and I give thanks for Your life that fills me with compassion, understanding, and peace.
- "I open my soul to You, and I give thanks for Your presence in my life and in the lives of the people I hold dear."

Militant Warfare Prayer to Close a Happy Day

- "It's almost time for me to go to sleep, Lord. But before I turn off the lights, I come to You in prayer, offering my thanks.
- "Yes, I am so grateful for this happy day You gave me. I really enjoyed it. For this is the day You have made, and I will rejoice in it.
- "Many good things happened to me as the hours went by, and I realize even more how nice it is to be alive.
- "Because today has been so wonderful, I feel very relaxed and peaceful as I get ready for bed.
- "Please help me to have a restful night, and when I wake up in the morning, may I be blessed with another happy day in my life.

- "Thank You for loving me. Good night, dear Lord."

Militant Warfare Prayer to Close a Difficult Day

- "I am very glad, dear Lord, that my bedtime has arrived.
- "God, this has been such a difficult day for me to get through.
- "My mind and body are so tired. It truly seems as though one problem after another has occurred today.
- "But I was able to keep going, thanks to Your loving help.
- "I need to rest now and to forget how trying this day has been for me.
- "Please bless me with a good night's sleep, and when morning comes, let me feel refreshed and renewed.
- "I pray that You will answer my prayer by making tomorrow a much better day for me. I love You. Good night, dear Lord."

Militant Warfare Prayer to Close a Busy Day

- "I have something to tell You, Lord, before I shut my eyes to go to sleep. I must say thank you.
- "Yes, I want to thank You for giving me the energy to get through today. Without You I don't know what would have happened.
- "I truly needed Your help, because this has been a very busy day for me. And You gave me help, just as I needed.

- "From morning until right now at bedtime, I have had so many things to do. But You helped me throughout the day to accomplish them.
- "And there were times when I wondered if I could get them done, but with You guiding me, I am happy to say that I did accomplish a great deal today.
- "Please watch over me as I sleep, and bless me with a peaceful night.
- "May I be rested to begin a brand-new day. Good night, dear Lord."

Militant Warfare Prayer to Close a Sad Day

- "I am very downhearted tonight, Lord. And I ask for Your help as I come to You in these prayerful moments at bedtime.
- "Things have happened today to make me feel so sad and blue. But even though my spirits are low, I still have faith in You.
- "How thankful I am to know that I can always count on Your love, so I pray that You will help me now in my time of sadness.
- "Uplift me and bring me comfort. Bless me with the courage to carry on. And may I rest well throughout this night.
- "For I want to face tomorrow with strength and clear thoughts. Good night, dear Lord."

Militant Warfare Prayer to Close a Successful Day

- "I feel content as I get ready for bed, Lord. And I believe this wonderful feeling is because of the 'good fortune' that came my way today.

- "Thank You for helping to make this day such a successful day in my life. It has given me hope that even better things are in store for me. I truly appreciate the many gifts I receive from You.
- "May I always be worthy of them. Please continue to stay by my side, leading me to even greater joy and success; and after this peaceful night of sleep, may tomorrow be another fine day in Your care.
- "Thank You so much. Good night, dear Lord."

Militant Warfare Prayer to Close a Holiday

- "Though the hours of this holiday celebration are almost gone, Lord, they surely will not be forgotten.
- "For today has provided me with such pleasant memories. I hope, too, that I will never forget how blessed I am by You.
- "Each wonderful thing You bring into my life is greatly appreciated. Please accept my thanks, which are indeed sincere.
- "I have to go to bed and rest now. But I want You to know my feelings as this holiday comes to a close.
- "May I sleep peacefully tonight and always in Your good care. Love of my life, good night, dear Lord."

Militant Warfare Prayer to be made whole in Jesus

- "Heavenly Father, I bow in worship and praise before You. I cover myself with the blood of the Lord Jesus Christ as my protection. I surrender myself to You, completely and unreservedly, in every area of my life.

- "I take a stand against all the workings of Satan that would hinder me in my prayer life. I address myself only to the true and living God and refuse any involvement of Satan in my prayer. Satan, I command you, in the name of the Lord Jesus Christ, to leave my presence, with all your demons.

- "I bring the blood of the Lord Jesus Christ between us, you wicked devil. The blood of Jesus surrounds me like a mighty wall that you cannot penetrate.

- "Heavenly Father, I worship You and give You praise. I recognize that You are worthy to receive all glory and honor and praise. I renew my allegiance to You and pray that the blessed Holy Spirit would enable me in this time of prayer.

- "I am thankful, heavenly Father, that You have loved me from past eternity and that You sent the Lord Jesus Christ into the world to die as my substitute. I am thankful that the Lord Jesus Christ came as my representative and that through Him You have completely forgiven me. You have adopted me into Your family; You have assumed all responsibility for me; You have given me eternal life; You have given me the perfect righteousness of the Lord Jesus Christ so that I am now justified.

- "I am thankful that in Him, You have made me complete and that You have offered Yourself to me to be my daily help and strength.

- "Heavenly Father, open my eyes that I might see how great You are and how complete Your provision is for this day. I am thankful that the victory the Lord Jesus Christ won for me on the cross and in His resurrection has been given to me and that I am seated with the Lord Jesus Christ in the heavenlies.

- "I take my place with Him in the heavenlies and recognize by faith that all wicked spirits and Satan himself are under my feet. I declare, therefore, that Satan and his wicked spirits are subject to me in the name of the Lord Jesus Christ.

- "I am thankful for the armor You have provided. I put on the girdle of truth, the breastplate of righteousness, the sandals of peace, and the helmet of salvation. I lift up the shield of faith against all the fiery darts of the enemy, and I take in my hand the sword of the Spirit, the Word of God. I choose to use Your Word against all the forces of evil in my life.

- "I put on this armor and live and pray in complete dependence upon You, blessed Holy Spirit. I am grateful, heavenly Father, that the Lord Jesus Christ spoiled all principalities and powers and made a show of them openly and triumphed over them in Himself. I claim all that victory for my life today.

- "I reject all the insinuations, accusations, and temptations of Satan. I affirm that the Word of God is true, and I choose to live today in the light of God's Word. I choose, heavenly Father, to live in obedience to You and in fellowship with You.

- "Open my eyes and show me the areas of my life that do not please You. Work in me to cleanse me from all ground that would give Satan a foothold against me. I do in every way stand in all that it means to be Your adopted child, and I welcome all the ministry of the Holy Spirit.

- "By faith and in dependence upon You, I put off the fleshly works of the evil one and stand in all the victory of the crucifixion where the Lord Jesus

Christ provided cleansing from the old nature. I put on Your holiness and stand in all the victory of the resurrection and the provision He has made for me to live above sin. Therefore, today I put off all forms of selfishness and put on the new nature with its love.

- "I put off all forms of fear and put on the new nature with its courage. I put off all forms of weakness and put on the new nature with its strength.

- "I put off all forms of lust and put on the new nature with its righteousness, purity, and honesty. I trust You to show me how to make this practical in my daily life. In every way, I stand in the victory of the ascension and glorification of the Lord Jesus Christ, whereby all the principalities and powers were made subject to Him.

- "I claim my place in Christ as victorious with Him over all the enemies of my soul. Blessed Holy Spirit, I pray that You would fill me. Come into my life; break down every idol and cast out every foe.

- "I am thankful, heavenly Father, for the expression of Your will for my daily life as You have shown me in Your Word. I, therefore, claim all the will of God for today. I am thankful that You have blessed me with all spiritual blessings in heavenly places in Christ Jesus.

- "I am thankful that You have begotten me unto a living hope by the resurrection of Jesus Christ from the dead. I am thankful that You have made a provision so that today I can live filled with the Spirit of God with love and joy and peace; with long-suffering, gentleness, and goodness; with meekness, faithfulness, and self-control in my life.

- "I recognize that this is Your will for me, and I therefore reject and resist all the endeavors of Satan and his wicked spirits to rob me of the will of God. I refuse in this day to believe my feelings, and I hold up the shield of faith against all the accusations, distortions, and insinuations that Satan would put into my mind.

- "I claim the fullness of the will of God for my life today. In the name of the Lord Jesus Christ, I completely surrender myself to You, heavenly Father, as a living sacrifice. I choose not to be conformed to this world. I choose to be transformed by the renewing of my mind, and I pray that You would show me Your will and enable me to walk in all the fullness of Your will today.

- "I am thankful, heavenly Father, that the weapons of our warfare are not carnal, but mighty through God to the pulling down of strongholds, to the casting down of imaginations and every high thing that exalts itself against the knowledge God, and to bringing every thought into obedience to the Lord Jesus Christ.

- "Therefore, in my own life today, I tear down the strongholds of Satan and smash the plans of Satan that have been formed against me. I tear down the strongholds of Satan against my mind, and I surrender my mind to You, blessed Holy Spirit.

- "I affirm, heavenly Father, that You have not given me the spirit of fear, but of power, and of love, and of a sound mind. I break and smash the strongholds of Satan formed against my emotions today, and I give my emotions to You. I smash the strongholds of Satan formed against my will today; I give my will to You and choose to make the right decisions of faith. I smash the strongholds of Satan formed against my body today; I give my body to You, recognizing that I am Your temple. I rejoice in Your mercy and goodness.

- "Heavenly Father, I pray that now and throughout this day, You would strengthen and enlighten me. Show me the way Satan is hindering and tempting me and lying and distorting the truth in my life. Enable me to be the kind of person that would please You. Enable me to be aggressive in prayer and faith.

- "Enable me to be aggressive mentally, to think about and practice Your Word, and to give You Your rightful place in my life. Again, I cover myself with the blood of the Lord Jesus Christ and pray that Your blessed Holy Spirit would bring all the work of the crucifixion, all the work of the resurrection, all the work of the glorification, and all the work of Pentecost into my life today.

- "I surrender myself to You. I refuse to be discouraged. You are the God of all hope. You have proven Your power by resurrecting Jesus Christ from the dead, and I claim in every way this victory over all the satanic forces in my life. I pray in the name of the Lord Jesus Christ, with thanksgiving and praise to You alone. Amen."

Militant Warfare Prayer for Forgiveness

Forgiveness is an act of the will, not a feeling. If you pray for a person, you can be assured that you have forgiven that person. To help accept an individual and open yourself to a particular person more, picture him with the Lord

Jesus and say to the Lord, "I love him because You love him. I forgive him because You forgive him."

- "Lord Jesus Christ, I ask today to forgive *everyone* in my life. I know that You will give me the strength to forgive, and I thank You that You love me more than I love myself and want my happiness more than I desire it for myself.
- "Father, I ask that You forgive me for the times when death, hard times, financial difficulties, or what I thought were punishments sent by You came into my family and I became bitter and resentful towards You, believing those who said, 'It's God's will.'
- "Purify my heart and mind today. Lord, I forgive *myself* for my sins, faults, and failings, for all that is bad in me or that I think is bad.
- "I forgive myself, and I accept Your forgiveness. I further forgive *myself* for taking Your name in vain, not worshiping You by attending church, for hurting my parents, getting drunk, for sins against purity, reading bad books, looking at bad movies, committing fornication and adultery. Also, I forgive *myself* for abortion, stealing, lying, defrauding, and hurting people's reputations. You have forgiven me today, and I forgive *myself*.
- "Thank You, Lord, for Your grace at this moment. I also forgive *myself* for any delving in superstition, using Ouija boards, reading horoscopes, going to witch doctors, using fortune-telling, or wearing lucky charms.
- "I reject all that superstition and choose You alone as my Lord and Savior. Fill me with Your Holy Spirit.

- "Lord, I truly forgive my *mother*. I forgive her for all the times she hurt me, resented me, was angry with me, and for all the times she punished me. I forgive her for the times she preferred my brothers and sisters to me. I forgive her for the times she told me I was dumb, ugly, stupid, the worst of the children, or that I cost the family a lot of money. For the times she told me I was unwanted, an accident, a mistake, or not what she expected, I forgive her.

- "Lord, I truly forgive my *father*. I forgive him for any nonsupport; for any lack of love, affection, or attention. I forgive him for any lack of time, for not giving me his companionship, for his drinking, for his arguing and fighting with my mother or the other children. For his severe punishments, for his desertion, for his being away from home, for his divorcing my mother, or for any running around, I do forgive him.

- "Lord, I extend forgiveness to my *sisters* and *brothers*. I forgive those who rejected me, lied about me, hated me, resented me, competed for my parents' love, hurt me, or physically harmed me. For those who were too severe on me, punished me, or made my life unpleasant in any way, I do forgive them.

- "Lord, I forgive my *spouse* for lack of love, affection, consideration, support, attention, or communication; for faults, failings, weaknesses, and those other acts or words that hurt or disturb me.

- "Jesus, I forgive my *children* for their lack of respect, obedience, love, attention, support, warmth, or understanding; for their bad habits, their falling away from the church, or any bad actions that disturb me, I also forgive them.

- "Lord God, I forgive my *in-laws*—my mother-in-law, father-in-law, son/daughter-in-law, and any other relatives by marriage—who treat my family with a lack of love. For all their words, thoughts, actions, or omissions that injure and cause pain, I forgive them.

- "Please help me to forgive my *relatives*—my grandmother and grandfather, aunts, uncles, and cousins—who may have interfered in our family, been possessive of my parents, caused confusion, or turned one parent against the other.

- "Jesus, help me to forgive my *co-workers* who are disagreeable or make life miserable for me. For those who push their work off on me, gossip about me, won't cooperate with me, or try to take my job, I do forgive them.

- "My *neighbors* need to be forgiven, Lord. For all their noise, letting their property run down, not tying up their dogs that run through my yard, not taking in their trash barrels, being prejudiced, and running down the neighborhood, I do forgive them.

- "I do forgive my pastor, elders, deacons, my *congregation,* and my *church* for their lack of support, affirmation, bad sermons, pettiness, lack of friendliness, not providing me or my family with the inspiration we needed, for any hurts they have inflicted on me or my family, even in the distant past, I forgive them today.

- "Lord, I forgive all those who are of different *persuasions,* those of opposite political views who have attacked me, ridiculed me, discriminated against me, made fun of me, or economically hurt me.

- "I forgive those of different religious *denominations* and *beliefs* who have harassed me, attacked me, argued with me, and forced their views on me or my family.

- "Those who have harmed me *ethnically,* discriminated against me, mocked me, made jokes about my race or nationality, hurt my family physically, emotionally, or economically, I do forgive them today.

- "Lord, I forgive all *professional people* who have hurt me in any way: doctors, nurses, lawyers, judges, politicians, and civil servants.

- "I forgive all service people: policemen, firemen, bus drivers, hospital workers, and especially repairmen who have taken advantage of me in their work.

- "Lord, I forgive my *employer* for not paying me enough money, for not appreciating my work, for being unkind and unreasonable with me, for being angry or unfriendly, for not promoting me, and for not complimenting me on my work.

- "Lord, I forgive both my present and past *schoolteachers* and *instructors.* For those who punished me, humiliated me, insulted me, treated me unjustly, made fun of me, called me dumb or stupid, or made me stay after school, I truly forgive them today.

- "Lord, I forgive my *friends* who have let me down, lost contact with me, did not support me, were not available when I needed help, borrowed money and did not return it, or gossiped about me.

- "Lord Jesus, I especially pray for the grace of forgiveness for the *one person* in life who has *hurt me the most.*
- "I forgive anyone whom I consider my greatest enemy, the one who is the hardest to forgive, or the one whom I said I would never forgive.
- "Lord, I beg pardon of all these people for the hurt I have inflicted on them, especially my mother and father, and my marriage partner.
- "I am especially sorry for the three greatest hurts I have inflicted on each of these.
- "Thank You, Jesus, that I am being freed of the evil of unforgiveness. Let Your Holy Spirit fill me with light, and let every dark area of my mind be enlightened."

Militant Warfare Prayer for Financial Breakthrough

- "Dear Jesus, I repent of any sin or disobedience of my ancestors that has allowed financial curse or hardship to prevail against me.
- "I destroy every satanic altar and covenant that is directly responsible for financial hardship and difficulties in my life.
- "I destroy the spirit of poverty that was inherited through the bloodline, and I bind all family curses of poverty. I break every satanic chain of poverty.
- "I renounce and reverse every financial curse, through the blood of the eternal covenant.
- "I bind and destroy the activities of anti-harvest forces.
- "I destroy all spiritual padlocks that lock out wealth from coming into my life, in Jesus' name.

- "I destroy every device of the enemy to divert my wealth through sickness, sudden death, accidents, and financial emergencies.
- "I erase, through the blood of Jesus Christ, every mark or handwriting of poverty on my life.
- "I command every leaking pocket, purse, and wallet to be sealed in Jesus' name.
- "I command the builders of financial roadblocks in my life to be arrested. I issue a warrant, pursue arrest, destroy, and terminate their assignments.
- "I pull down every financial roadblock and command the crooked places to be made straight, valleys to be exalted, and mountains to be brought low so that my financial miracles can arrive to me with speed.
- "I command my financial deserts and wildernesses to be turned into springs and pools of water.
- "I bind every spirit of unfruitfulness. I command my barren ground to be healed, and I declare that my labors shall not be in vain.
- "I destroy the operations of the spirit of indebtedness over my life, in Jesus' name.
- "With the fire of God, I destroy every garment of poverty that the enemy has put on me. I command new garments of favor, wealth, and prominence to be divinely put on me.
- "I pray, dear Lord, that You would anoint my eyes to see Your opportunities and provision.
- "I now renew my commitment to You, dear God, in the area of tithes, offerings, and vows.
- "I command every closed heaven to be opened and to release an outpouring of the blessings of God upon my life. Free the channels of my financial blessings, dear Lord.

- "I release the anointing for wealth and prosperity to flow mightily upon my life. I declare that from now on I will enter into my season of financial conquest and triumph.
- "I command into manifestation my seasons of divine opportunity, money, and blessing to be restored with interest. I demand wholeness in every dimension in my life, in Jesus' name."

Militant Warfare Prayer for Your Business or Job

Pray this prayer militantly to destroy every anti-prosperity force against your business or job.

- "Lord Jesus, help me to submit to Your will every day of my life.
- "Cause me to be spiritually and mentally alert in my place of work and business.
- "Let all my plans and purposes for my business bring honor and glory to You, O Lord Jesus.
- "Father, let Your angels lift up my business on their hands so that it does not strike its foot against a stone, in the name of Jesus.
- "Let all decisions made in my business be originated by You and the Holy Spirit, in Jesus' name.
- "Let the influence of the Holy Ghost be upon every person in this set-up, in the name of Jesus.
- "Let my business continue to grow and expand, in the name of Jesus.
- "O Lord, give me direction and guidance at all times on this company/store (you name it).
- "Let the business prosper and have good success, in the name of Jesus.

- "Father, let my path grow brighter and brighter until it reaches the full light of the day, in the name of Jesus.
- "I bind every spirit of uncertainty and confusion, in the mighty name of Jesus.
- "I walk out of the realm of failure into the arena of success, in the wonderful name of Jesus.
- "I remove my business from the dominion of the powers of darkness.
- "In Jesus' name, I ask the Father for sufficient legions of the holy angels to bind all satanic forces in my business and the air overhead so they will be unable to interfere in any way with its prosperity.
- "I take authority over and bind the strongman of financial failure.
- "I command the curse and ordination of debt in this business to be nullified, in Jesus' name.
- "Lord, anoint my brain to prosper after the order of Bazaleel, the son of Uri, the son of Hur, of the tribe of Judah.
- "Let the anointing of fire be in all my writings, thinking, and organization.
- "I stamp out every spirit of anger, lack of cooperation, wrong judgments, contentions, and disloyalty among staff, in Jesus' name
- "Let this business become a channel of blessings and a foundation of life for other businesses, in Jesus' name.
- "Let the shower of financial revival fall upon this business.
- "Lord, anoint all letters for help emanating from me to go forth accompanied by divine favor, angelic transportation, and positive results.

- "I reverse every curse that has been issued against this business, in Jesus' name.
- "Father, in the name of Jesus, assign ministering spirits to go forth to minister on my behalf and bring in trade.
- "Lord, give me the wisdom and ability to understand righteousness and fair dealing in business.
- "Lord, give me grace to remain diligent in acquiring knowledge and skill in areas in which I am inexperienced.
- "Let my business bring forth and prosper, in the name of Jesus.
- "I declare that the devil will have no control over my finances, in the name of Jesus.
- "I declare that the devil will not be able to steal my finances, in the name of Jesus.
- "Lord, give unto me godly counsel, knowledge, and wisdom for managing my finances.
- "Let those who would defraud or cheat me be put to shame and confusion, in the name of Jesus.
- "Let those who would plan to steal from my business be put to shame and confusion, in the name of Jesus.
- "Father, make Your face to shine upon me and enlighten me, and be gracious unto me, in the name of Jesus.
- "Lord, bestow Your favor upon me, in the name of Jesus.
- "Father, make me a blessing to my family, neighbors, and business associates, in the name of Jesus.
- "Lord, pour out upon me the spirit of favor.
- "Father, give me knowledge and skill in all learning and wisdom, in the name of Jesus.

- "Father, bring me to find favor, compassion, and loving-kindness with all my business contacts, in the name of Jesus.
- "Lord, cause me to obtain favor in the sight of all who look upon me, in Jesus' name."

Militant Warfare Prayer for Deliverance from Demons

Deliverance Prayer

- "Father, I come before You in *Jesus'* name, and I thank You for giving me all power and all authority over all demons. I cover myself in the blood of *Jesus*.
- "I cover all my family members in the blood of *Jesus*. I thank You for Your giant warring angels that are surrounding us, protecting us from all harm of the enemy.
- "I take my authority and attack from the third heaven, and I bind the strongman over my mind, will, emotions, and over my home, in *Jesus'* name.
- "I command you to leave this area now, in *Jesus'* name. I bind up every demon that was sent to me, transferred to me, or followed me, and I command you to come out of my conscious, subconscious, unconscious mind and all parts of my body, will, emotions, and personality, in *Jesus'* name."

Another Deliverance Prayer

- "Dear God, in the name of Jesus and according to Romans 10:9, I confess with my lips that *Jesus* is

Lord, and in my heart I believe that You raised Him from the dead.

- "According to Luke 13:3, I repent of my past sins. I admit and confess that I have sinned, and I believe that You are faithful and just to cleanse me from all unrighteousness.

- "I call upon You, Lord *Jesus,* to cleanse me from all sin and unrighteousness by Your blood (1 John 1:7).

- "And as Your Word says in Romans 10:13, everyone who calls upon the name of the Lord will be saved.

- "I confess and repent of occult practices such as witchcraft, fortune-telling, horoscopes, astrology, water-witching, etc.

- "I renounce all occult practices and Satan, and I break all curses associated with those occult practices.

- "According to Galatians 3:13, 'Christ purchased our freedom [redeeming us] from the curse [doom] of the Law [and its condemnation] by [Himself] becoming a curse for us, for it is written [in the Scriptures], "Cursed is everyone who hangs on a tree" (is crucified)' (Deut. 21:23).

- "I confess and repent of all sins listed in Deuteronomy 27 and 28 and break the curses associated with those sins.

- "I confess and repent of my iniquities and my fathers' iniquities according to Leviticus 26:40, and I break the curses associated with those iniquities.

- "I break and loose myself from all evil soul ties with my mother, father, brothers, sisters, spouses, former spouses, former sex partners, pastors, churches, friends, etc.

- "Lord *Jesus*, I forgive my mother, father, brothers, sisters, and anyone else who has ever hurt me, including all whites, blacks, Indians, etc. (Matt. 6:15; 18:21– 22, 35; Luke 11:4 [Lord's Prayer]).
- "I break and loose myself and my family from all curses that have been and are being placed upon me and my family, including any demons being sent to us; curses of witchcraft; psychic thoughts or prayers; ungodly intercessory prayers; all words spoken in anger, hurt, sorrow, or bitterness; all incense being burned for or against us; in *Jesus'* name. Amen!"

Militant Warfare Prayer Against Weather Demons

Believe it or not, foul weather can be caused by demons, which means we have authority over them in that area too. Time and time again, we have prayed against severe weather, and it has either stopped in its tracks or headed the other way. It must be noted, however, that if God wants to allow your neighbor's property to be damaged, the storm will come through; but your property can be safeguarded, *if* you are right with the Lord.

Job 1:19 tells us of a great whirlwind from the desert that killed Job's children. Acts 27:14 tells us of a typhoon-type wind that came upon Paul at sea.

- "In the name of *Jesus*, I bind all demons that cause hail, excess heat and cold, lingering domes, fire, earthquakes, tornadoes, lightning, damaging winds, floods, hurricanes, and bad weather of all kinds.

- "I bind Chango, Oxun, Euroclydon, Baal, Seir, Leviathan, Hadadrimmon, Amurr, Basilisk, and all other demon spirits.
- "Father, I ask You to send Your warring angels (Matt. 26:53) into the heavenlies to do battle with these demons, to knock them off their thrones, to take their crowns from their heads, and to write on their foreheads that they have been defeated by the Lord *Jesus* Christ.
- "Father, I ask that You send the warring angels to block these demons from coming into my city, state, or county.
- "I ask for warring angels to be placed around my property and home for protection from these demons.
- "In *Jesus'* name, I cover my property, home, possessions, and family in the blood of *Jesus*. Amen."

Militant Warfare Prayer Against Witchcraft

- "Father, In *Jesus'* name, I break and loose myself from all witchcraft curses and evil and demons being sent to me and my family.
- "As your war club (Jer. 51:20–23) and weapon of war, I break into pieces the walls of protection that the Satanists and witches have put up; and I return the evil and demons back to them.
- "As Exodus 22:18 says, I send the judgment of God to the Satanists and witches sending anything my way, in *Jesus'* name.
- "I heap coals from the altar of God upon their foreheads, in *Jesus'* name.

- "I cover my family and myself with the blood of *Jesus* and ask for warring angels to be placed around us for protection.
- "I break and loose us from psychic power, thoughts, and prayers.
- "I break and loose us from words spoken in hurt, anger, sorrow, or bitterness.
- "I break and loose us from the power of incense and candles being burned on our behalves.
- "I break and loose us from ungodly intercessory prayers, in *Jesus'* name. Amen."

Militant Warfare Prayer Against Financial Crisis

Having in your home unicorns; statues of Buddha, elephants, or frogs; a statue of a tiger representing Durga (an Indian god); Chinese bamboo plants; or an Italian horn can cause financial problems. This can be statues or anything else.

- "Father, in *Jesus'* name, I bind all demons that would cause me to have job failure or money failure.
- "I bind all demons that would keep me from receiving all money, possessions, inheritance, jobs, promotions, bonuses, or raises that are rightfully mine.
- "In *Jesus'* name, I command the demons to return these to me sevenfold. Father, I ask that You send your angels out to gather these and bring them to me, in *Jesus'* name.
- "I loose the blessings of Deuteronomy 28 upon me, in *Jesus'* name. Amen."

Militant Warfare Prayer for Health

Be sure and cast out all of these demons: spirit of infirmity, sickness, disease, illnesses of all kinds, etc.

- "Father, in *Jesus'* name, I bind all demons of infirmity, sickness, disease, and illnesses of all kinds. I loose myself from these demons, and I loose the healing virtue of Jesus Christ into my body."

Militant Warfare Prayer for Sleep

- "Father, in *Jesus'* name, I bind all demons of the night, nightmares, bad dreams, torment, sleeplessness, and torture.
- "I command these demons to loose me and come out of me, and I ask that You protect my mind while I sleep, in *Jesus'* name."

Militant Warfare Prayer at the Breakfast Table

- "Dear heavenly and gracious Father, thank You for a good day, for protecting us against powers, principalities, evil forces in this world, and spiritual wickedness in high places.
- "Now, Lord, we apply the blood over ourselves and bind Satan away from us, our jobs and our clients, church, our children's school, our yard, our house, our possessions, and everything that we have any part in.
- "Lord, send Your angels to minister unto us, build a ring of Holy Ghost fire around us, and cover us with Your blood.

- "We pray for the United States of America and Israel, the Christians and the Jews, the churches that worship Jesus in spirit and truth.
- "We ask for courage, understanding, wisdom, and strength.
- "We pray especially for the leaders and ask a double portion for our families.
- "We ask divine favor with You in accordance with the Holy Word of God, with each other and those we come into contact with today.
- "We confess that this is the day that the Lord has made. We will rejoice and be glad in it; for God has not given us a spirit of fear, but of power, love, and a sound mind.
- "He that is in us is greater than he that is in the world. If God be for us, who can be against us?
- "You have given us power over all the power of the enemy, and we intend to exercise it by the leadership of the Holy Spirit.
- "Now, Lord, we ask that You lead, guide, direct, and protect us. Let us walk in Your perfect will; we yield ourselves to You today.
- "We thank You for our food, clothing, and shelter, and for everything that You have done for us, known and unknown.
- "We ask You to bless this food to our bodies; purify and cleanse it so that our temples will be fit for the Holy Spirit to reside in.
- "All these things we ask in the blessed name of Jesus Christ, our Lord, Master, and Savior."

Militant Warfare Prayer for the Day

- "Dear Lord, we ask You to forgive us of our sins; teach us and show us so that we will be pleasing in Your sight.
- "We pray this day for ourselves, our family, friends, neighbors, and relatives, and for the leadership of the Holy Spirit.
- "We thank You for each other this day, and most of all for You. We pray for our relatives and friends, our Christian brothers and sisters.
- "We pray for those who labor in the field of deliverance, for their families, churches, and ministries, that You would give them a triple portion of courage, understanding, wisdom, and strength.
- "We pray for the army of the Lord, that it would grow strong and mighty and be valiant and do exploits in the name of Jesus Christ.
- "We pray that deliverance would come to the forefront of Christianity. We pray for those that we have ministered to, for their families, churches, and ministries, that they would go on with the Lord.
- "We pray for all men everywhere, that they would come into the saving knowledge of Jesus Christ.
- "We pray for the fivefold ministry on our families, churches, and ministries. We pray for our pastors and for our business.
- "We pray Your blessings on these. We bind up all powers, principalities, and evil forces in this world, and spiritual wickedness in high places.
- "We loose the powers of God: warring angels, ministering angels, the Holy Spirit, and the seven-

fold Spirit of God to come down and do a mighty battle on earth today.

- "We bind up every force of evil and loose every force of good that we have the power and authority to do, in Jesus' name.
- "We thank you, Lord, for power and authority over the enemy, and for the use of the name of Jesus Christ, for it's in His name we pray. Amen."

Militant Warfare Prayer for a Healthy and In-Shape Body

Using this prayer is great, but you must remember that wisdom is needed to help keep your body in shape. Watch what you eat and how you take care of yourself. It is very important to take care of your body, because it is the temple of the Holy Spirit.

Declarations of Faith

- "I command my body to weigh _____ pounds. I command every cell to function in wholeness.
- "Every biogenetic curse of addiction, I break right now, in Jesus' name. My DNA is correct and functions in line with God's Word.
- "Every generational curse of obesity and all other curses affecting my weight are now broken, in Jesus' name.
- "I command every spirit of gluttony, bulimia, anorexia, sugar addiction, overindulgence, compulsion, addiction, craving, lack of self-control, anxiety, depression, anger, unworthiness, deformity, unbelief, depression, oppression, self-hatred, hatred of

my body, ugliness, rejection, rebellion, inconsistency, deception, failure, fear, intimidation, and all other connected and related spirits not of the Lord Jesus Christ to come out now, in the name and by the blood of Jesus Christ.

- "You are not allowed to dwell in or around, or attach to me in any way. It is finished; be now gone, in Jesus' name.

- "My body is whole and healthy. I eat healthy food. I exercise physically, mentally, spiritually, and emotionally on a level of maximum efficiency.

- "I am not moved by what I see, for faith is the substance of things hoped for but not yet seen.

- "I can do all things through Christ who strengthens me. I love and respect my body and call it holy, as the Lord my God is holy.

- "My metabolism; glandular system; blood-sugar level; respiratory, cardiovascular, digestive, neuromuscular, and all other systems of my body; every cell; and every organ function as they were created to in perfect harmony and balance.

- "I walk in the wholeness of Jesus Christ. I have outward and inward beauty. The beauty of Christ radiates from my very presence.

- "The Jesus who is in me is beautiful, and the fragrance of the Lord follows me wherever I go. I am the bride of Christ, pure, spotless, and blameless before Him.

- "The favor of the Lord rests upon me and is unconditionally abounding toward me in every situation and circumstance.

- "God and man love and accept me. I am accepted in the beloved.

- "Jesus has plans and a hope for my future, and I will fulfill every inch, every centimeter of what He has for me.
- "Satan is bound from interfering with the divine path of destiny that the Lord Jesus Christ has called me to.
- "I will no longer let fear, intimidation, rejection, or any other thing stand in my way.
- "I run the race with a victor's crown on my head and feet that are swift to reach the high calling God has placed upon my life.
- "I walk on high places in the power of the Holy Spirit, who resides big in me.
- "I am violently and forcefully taking back everything the enemy has stolen from me.
- "All of Satan's plans and assignments are canceled. I am fully equipped and equipping others in the art of warfare.
- "The high praises of God are upon my lips, and I stand with a two-edged sword in my hand, slicing into and pushing back the forces of darkness.
- "The weapons of my warfare are not carnal, but mighty through God to the pulling down of strongholds.
- "I am sharpened as iron sharpens iron. I have the mind of Christ and hold the thoughts, feelings, and intentions of His heart.
- "I take every thought captive to the obedience of Christ Jesus my Lord. Every fiery dart directed at my mind is quenched by the shield of faith.
- "I do not entertain vain imaginations. I think only on the glorious and lovely things of God.

- "The words of my mouth are words that are creative and bring life to all who hear them. He has anointed me to heal the brokenhearted and set the captives free.
- "I am more than a conqueror by the word of my testimony and the blood of the Lamb.
- "I am fully anointed. I am a chosen one. I am a general with the highest rank in the Lord's army. When I pray, demons tremble and cannot remain in my presence, for I am pure terror and dread to the enemy's camp.
- "Demonic spirits run and flee as I approach and do not manifest in my presence. I am the walking, talking Word of God in human form.
- "The resurrection power of Christ resides in me. Signs and wonders follow me; and I will do greater works than these because Jesus said I could, and I will, in His name.
- "The love of God is shed abroad in my heart for all men. God's love for me is unconditional.
- "God is continually pouring out favor and blessing upon my life and the lives of my family members.
- "We live in the prosperity and wisdom of Solomon, the freedom and favor of David, and the faith of Abraham, our forefather.
- "Goodness and mercy follow us as the angels of the Lord God protect and encourage us at every turn. We hear the voice of the Lord; divine appointments, friendships, business opportunities, ministry connections, mentors, and higher levels of wisdom, revelation, and understanding come to us.
- "Finances and resources flow to us easily and without interruption. They flow like the river of God.

- "I undo any ungodly blockages preventing me from receiving what the Lord is trying to get to me. My family and I are positioned for the purposes of the Lord Jesus Christ.
- "We are in the right places at the right times. No weapon formed against us will ever prosper, and every tongue that rises against us, Thou shalt condemn.
- "Word curses of others shall bear no fruit in our lives. They are returned immediately to the demonic source from whence they came. We are free from all curses, for Jesus Christ became a curse for us at Calvary.
- "Therefore, we are abundantly supplied, divinely healthy, completely beautiful, and fully restored.
- "We are whole and thriving, as trees planted by the divine waters of life.
- "Jesus is the way, the truth, and the life. We abide in the Lord Jesus Christ and are fruitful.
- "We have a Joshua-Caleb spirit and see that all things are possible for us because we believe.
- "We go forward and possess the Promised Land by the power of Your might, dear Jesus.
- "It is not by our might or by our power, but it is by Your Spirit. We see the heavenly gates opening to us as we use the keys to the house of David and enter into the mansion of Your holy presence and the throne room of Your glory.
- "Holy, holy, holy is the Lord God almighty. All God's promises are yes and amen."

Militant Warfare Prayer for Daily Protection

- "I put on tender mercies, kindness, humility, meekness, and long-suffering; and I put on love, the bond of perfection.
- "I welcome the peace of God to rule my heart.
- "I allow the Word of God to dwell in my heart richly in all wisdom, teaching and admonishing others in psalms and hymns and spiritual songs, singing with grace in my heart to the Lord.
- "Whatever I do, I do in word and in deed in the name of Jesus, giving thanks to God the Father through Him.
- "I put on Christ because I have been baptized in Him. I put on the Lord Jesus as a garment.
- "I put on the breastplate of faith and love.
- "I put on mercy and truth around my neck.
- "I put on the armor of light.
- "I place on myself the mind of Christ. I let this mind (the mind of Christ) be in me.
- "I meditate on Your Word, day and night. You are faithful to perform Your Word. You will bring it to completion. You are faithful to complete the work You have begun in me and my life.
- "Let the meditation of my heart and the words of my mouth be pleasing unto You, O Lord. I will open my mouth, and You will fill it.
- "I place a guard on my mouth. I commit my mouth to You, Lord, that I might not sin against You.
- "You, Lord, are seated high above all authority, power, dominion, and might. Nothing is too difficult for You.

- "I place the armor of righteousness on my right and left hands.
- "I put on strength. I clothe myself with strength for the battle. You are looking for a pure heart, whose heart You can strengthen.
- "I thank You for a shield of favor about me.
- "I plead the blood over my body, mind, will, soul, and emotions. I repent of all sins. I will not fear the arrow by day or the terror by night.
- "I put on the garment of salvation. I am clothed with salvation.
- "I put on the helmet of hope.
- "I put on the robe of righteousness.
- "I put on the blue ephod.
- "I ask for the fear of the Lord, which is the beginning of wisdom.
- "I ask for the spirit of wisdom, knowledge, understanding, and revelation.
- "I am anointed, appointed, called, marked, chosen, beloved, accepted, and not rejected, in Jesus' name.
- "I put on as a helmet the hope of salvation.
- "Help me, Lord, to be sober and vigilant, watchful in the Spirit, and aware of the enemy, the devil. Wake me up, spiritually.
- "I rule and reign with Christ Jesus.
- "Lord, You cover my head; You have covered my head in the day of battle.
- "The Word is my shield and buckler.
- "I loose myself from the bonds of my neck. I tie down my enemies in the spirit realm. I reverse the words of those who curse me, send evil against me, and send evil against the work of the Lord. I send

all evil back to them seven times, in the name of Jesus.

- "May they be brought to their knees and to repentance by the Lord Jesus, that they may be saved, healed, filled, and delivered, in Jesus' mighty name. I reverse every assignment, trap, snare, wile, and evil plan or attack against me from Satan and his angels, demons, imps, principalities, rulers of the darkness, powers, spiritual hosts of wickedness in the heavenly places, or spirits of any kind. I silence them and their words or curses.

- "I clothe them with confusion as with a mantle. I cancel all assignments against me. I make all word curses null and void.

- "I ask the Lord to send legions of angels to minister to me, protect me, battle for me, minister healing and restoration, and to surround me, in the name of Jesus.

- "I love, bless, and forgive those who persecute me and say all manner of evil against me for the sake of Your righteousness.

- "Help me, Lord, to be strong in You and in Your power, to exercise the authority over the devil that You have given me, to stand against the devil, to wrestle and do warfare, to put on my armor daily, to pray without ceasing, to intercede, and to fight the good fight of faith. Amen."

Militant Warfare Prayer for Every Day

- "Dear Lord, I thank You for this day. I thank You for my being able to see and to hear this morning.

I'm blessed because You are a forgiving God and an understanding God.

- "You have done so much for me, and You keep on blessing me. Forgive me this day, for I have sinned. I ask now for Your forgiveness.

- "Keep me safe from all danger and harm. Let me start this day with a new attitude and plenty of gratitude.

- "Let me make the best of each and every day and give my best in all that is put before me.

- "Clear my mind so that I can hear from You. Broaden my mind so that I can accept all things that are of You. Let me not whine and whimper about things over which I have no control.

- "Let me continue to see sin through Your eyes and acknowledge it as evil. And when I sin, let me repent and confess with my mouth my wrongdoing and receive the forgiveness of God.

- "And when this world closes in on me, let me remember Jesus' example to slip away and find a quiet place to pray. It's the best response when I'm pushed beyond my limits. I know that when I can't pray out loud, You listen to my heart.

- "Continue to use me to do Thy will. Continue to bless me so that I may be a blessing to others. Keep me strong so that I may help the weak and unsaved.

- "Keep me uplifted so that I may have words of encouragement for others. I pray for those who are lost and can't find their way. I pray for those who are misjudged and misunderstood.

- "I pray for those who refuse to share a word from You. I pray for those who don't know You intimately.

- "I pray for those who will only read this and not speak this aloud in their own lives. I pray for those who will delete this without sharing it with others. I pray for those who don't believe, but I thank You that I believe.
- "I believe that You change people, and I pray for all my sisters and brothers, for each and every family member in their households. I pray for peace, love, and joy in their homes so that they are out of debt and all their needs met.
- ""I pray that every eye that reads this knows there is no problem, circumstance, or situation greater than You, Lord. Every battle is in Your hands for You to fight.
- I pray that these words will be received into the hearts of every eye that sees them and every mouth that confesses them willingly."

Miscellaneous Warfare Prayers

And pray in the Spirit on all occasions with all kinds of prayers and requests. With this in mind, be alert and always keep on praying for all the saints.

— Ephesians 6:18

Be always on the watch, and pray that you may be able to escape all that is about to happen, and that you may be able to stand before the Son of Man.

— Luke 21:36

Everything in life needs to be renewed. What would your home look like if you never attended to it, repainted it, or cleaned it? You must renew your faith and commitment to the Lord and keep a checklist of your life, making sure everything is in order and not out of order. Renounce anything that needs to be renounced, and seek forgiveness. Don't allow Satan any foothold in your life.

Everyday Prayers

- "Lord, Even now I lift my eyes toward You. Jesus' grace and truth are realized in You.

- "Grant me grace that the truth of Your message will change my life and compel me in unrelenting love to You. In Jesus' name, amen."

- "Lord, I thank You for helping me to not grow weary in well-doing! When I am tempted to get tired, help me to remember that the manifestation of my faith and hope is just around the corner.
- "I ask Your Spirit to give me the strength to stay strong regardless of the length of the battle—and to keep fighting until the battle is finally finished and the victory has been won!
- "I pray this prayer in Jesus' name! Amen."

- "Father, I thank You for Your hand of protection upon me, my family, and friends for this coming New Year. Father, in the name of Jesus, I thank You that You watch over Your Word to perform it.
- " I thank You that my family, friends, and I dwell in the secret place of the Most High and that we remain stable and fixed under the shadow of the Almighty, whose power no foe can withstand.
- "I cover my family, friends, and myself with the precious blood of Jesus, Your Son, thus keeping us safe from the hideous snares of Satan and all his cohorts.
- "Father, You are our refuge and our fortress. No evil shall befall us, no accident shall overtake us, nor shall any plague or calamity come near our homes.
- "I release ministering angels to go forth and to encompass me, my family, and friends, to accompany and defend and preserve us in all our ways

of obedience and service. The angels are encamped around us.

- "I bind the devil from trying to influence them in any way this day. Shelter us in the palm of Your hand and save our homes from all storms. Keep us close to Your heart.

- "Father, You are our confidence, firm and strong. You keep our feet from being caught in a trap or hidden danger. When we lie down, You will give me, my family, and friends peaceful sleep. Father, You give this family safety and ease us. Jesus is our safety! In Jesus' name, amen."

- "Lord I pray for an increase of the anointing, love, and compassion. I know that promotion comes from You (Ps. 75:6–7), and I know that You are a rewarder of them that diligently seek You (Heb. 11:6).

- "Because of Your favor, Lord, I expect miraculous increase in every area of my life.

- "And I am a thousand times better from this moment on" (Deut.1:11). In Jesus' name, amen."

- "Father, please forgive me for not loving as I should. Your Word says that I am made in Your image; therefore, it is my desire to love as You do.

- "Right now I tap into the anointing to change, which is made available to me through Your love.

- "I pray that the atmosphere of my life, my home, my church, and my place of work would change as a result of Your love demonstrated through me. Let it begin today. In Jesus' name, I pray. Amen."

A Great Prayer Before Starting Your Day

- "Heavenly Father, I bow in worship and praise before You. I cover myself with the blood of Jesus Christ and claim the protection of the blood for my family, my finances, my home, my spirit, my soul, and my body. I surrender myself completely to You in every area of my life.

- "I take a stand against all the workings of the devil that would try and hinder me and my family from best serving You.

- "I address myself only to the true and living God, who has all power and control over everything.

- "Satan, I command you and all your demon forces of darkness, in the name of the Lord Jesus Christ, to leave my presence. I bring the blood of Jesus Christ between you and my family, my home, my finances, my spirit, my soul, and my body. In Jesus' name, I pray this.

- "I declare, therefore, that Satan and his wicked spirits are subject to me in the name of the Lord Jesus Christ. Furthermore, in my own life today, I destroy and tear down all the strongholds of Satan and smash the plans of Satan that have been formed against me and my family.

- "I tear down the strongholds of the devil against my mind, and I surrender my mind to you, blessed Holy Spirit.

- "I affirm, heavenly Father, that You have not given me the spirit of fear, but of power and of love and of a sound mind (2 Tim. 1:7).

- "Therefore, I resist the spirit of fear, in the name of Jesus, the Son of the living God, and I refuse to fear, refuse to doubt, refuse to worry, because I have authority (power) over all the power of the enemy, and nothing shall by any means hurt me (Luke 10:19).

- "I claim complete and absolute victory over the forces of darkness, in the name of Jesus, and I bind the devil and command him to loose my peace, joy, prosperity—both for me and every member of my family, for the glory of God. By *faith,* I call it done. I break and smash the strongholds of Satan formed against my emotions today and give my emotions to You, Lord Jesus.

- "I destroy the strongholds of Satan against my body today, and I give my body to You, Lord Jesus, realizing that I am the temple of the Holy Ghost (1 Cor. 3:16; 6:19-20).

- "Again, I cover myself with the blood of the Lord Jesus Christ and pray that the Holy Ghost would bring all the work of the crucifixion, all the work of the resurrection, all the work of the ascension, and all the work of restoration of the Lord Jesus Christ into my life today.

- "I surrender my life and possessions to You. I refuse to fear, worry, or be discouraged, in the name of Jesus. I will not hate, envy, or show any type of bitterness toward my brothers, sisters, or my enemies, but I will *love* them with the love of God shed abroad in my heart by the Holy Ghost.

- "Open my eyes and show me the areas of my life that do not please You, and give me the strength, grace, and wisdom to remove any sin or weight that would prevent Your close fellowship.

- "Work in me to cleanse me from all ground that would give the devil a foothold against me. I claim in every way the victory of the cross over all satanic forces in my life.
- "I pray in the name of the Lord Jesus Christ with thanksgiving, and I welcome all the ministry of the Holy Spirit. In the name and power of the blood of Jesus, amen."

- "I have power to tread on serpents and scorpions and over *all the power* of the enemy, *and nothing shall by any means hurt me!* I have power over all devils to cast them out.
- "I can lay hands on the sick, and they shall recover. I am more than a conqueror through Jesus Christ. I can do all things through Christ. I confess the many benefits of Calvary.
- "Bless the Lord, O my soul, and forget not all his *benefits:* who forgives *all* my iniquities, who heals *all* my diseases.
- "Who redeems my life from destruction, who crowns me with loving-kindness and tender mercy, who satisfies my mouth with good things that my strength is renewed.
- "All my sins are forgiven! All my diseases are healed! My life is preserved and strong in God! I am crowned with His mercy! In Jesus' name, amen!"

Another Powerful Warfare Prayer for the Day

- "Gracious God, I acknowledge that You are worthy of all honor, glory, and praise. I am thankful for the victorious work of Your Son, Jesus Christ, at

Calvary for me. I appreciate His victory for me now, as I willingly surrender every area of my life to Your will.

- "Thank You for the forgiveness and righteousness that has been given to me as Your adopted child. I trust in Your protection and provision daily. I know that Your love for me never ceases.

- "I rejoice in Your victory, my Lord, over all the principalities and powers in the heavenlies. In faith I stand in Your victory and commit myself to live obediently for You, my King.

- "I desire that my fellowship with You become greater. Reveal to me those things that grieve You and enable the enemy to secure an advantage in my life. I need the Holy Spirit's powerful ministry in my life, bringing conviction of sin and repentance of heart, strengthening my faith, and increasing perseverance in resisting temptation.

- "Help me to die to self and walk in the victory of the new creation You have provided for me. Let the fruits of the Spirit flow out of my life so that You will be glorified through my life.

- "I know that it is Your will that I should stand firm and resist all of the enemy's work against me. Help me to discern the attacks upon my thoughts and emotions. Enable me to stand upon Your Word and resist all the accusations, distortions, and condemnations that are hurled against me.

- "It is my desire to be transformed through the renewing of my mind so that I will not compromise with the ways of the world or yield to the enemy's attacks but be obedient to Your will.

- "I draw upon those spiritual resources that You have provided me, and I attack the strongholds and plans of the enemy that have been put in place against me. I command, in the name of Jesus Christ, that the enemy completely release my mind, will, emotions, and body. They have been yielded to the Lord, and I belong to Him.

- "Lord, enable me to become the person You created me to be. Help me as I pray to be strong in faith. Show me how to apply Your Word in my life each day. I know that I wear the full armor of God when I am committed to and stand firmly upon Your Word. I want You to have the supreme place in my life.

- "I surrender myself completely to You, Lord. You are always faithful, and You extend Your grace to me constantly, even when I do not realize it. I claim Your promise of forgiveness and cleansing in its fullness. In faith I receive the victory today that You have already put in place for me. I do this in the name of Jesus Christ, my Savior, with a grateful heart. In the name and power of the blood of Jesus, amen."

- "Lord Jesus, by the Holy Spirit's power, help me to remember and quicken my mind. Heavenly Father, in the name of Jesus Christ, I renounce Satan, bind and break the power and effects of his activities, and take back all legal ground and holds that Satan feels he has in my life for any reason.

- "Father, in Jesus' name, I recognize and renounce my involvement and participation in the following areas: _____ (name the areas). I renounce them, in Jesus' name. Amen."

I Confess I Am Not afraid!

- "Though I walk through the valley of the shadow of death I will fear no evil! I *fear not,* for Thou art with me.
- "I am not dismayed, for Thou art my God. Thou art helping me. Thou art strengthening me. Thou art upholding me with Thy right hand!
- "Thou hast not given me the spirit of fear, but of power, love, and a sound mind.
- "I have the spirit of *power* in me. I have the spirit of *love* in me.
- "I have the spirit of a *sound mind* in me.
- "Over me is the *blood of the Lamb.* The Lord goes before me. Jesus is *in* me!
- "The angel of the Lord encamps around me. Underneath me are the everlasting arms of God!
- "And *goodness* and *mercy* follow me all the days of my life. Hallelujah! Fear has no place in my life!"

Taking Authority over the Mind

- "In the name of Jesus, I come against the strongholds and every high thing in my mind.
- "I cast down those reasonings, those strongholds, vain imaginations, and every high thing that exalts itself against the knowledge of God.
- "I release my mind to the obedience of Christ. I loose it to be reconciled to God in every area of my life. In the name of Jesus, I pray. Amen."

Renunciation and Affirmation Prayer

- "In the name of the Lord Jesus Christ, as a redeemed child of God, I come to You, Lord, purchased by the blood of the Lord Jesus Christ.
- "I here and now renounce, revoke, and cancel all consent, sin, and any ground lost or given to Satan, and any occult involvement ever lost or given knowingly or unknowingly to any demon powers by me, my husband (wife), my parents, or my ancestors.
- "I do it now by claiming complete forgiveness and cleansing in the blood of the Lord Jesus Christ.
- "I also renounce, revoke, and cancel the devil and all his works, including all my spiritistic bondage.
- "I now claim and take back all the ground ever lost or given to evil spirits by my husband (wife), my parents, my ancestor, and myself.
- "In the name of the Lord Jesus Christ, I now command these evil spirits to depart from me and go to the pit of hell, never to return.
- "I also surrender and dedicate myself completely— spirit, soul, body, mind, will, and emotions—to the Lord Jesus Christ.
- "I pray that You would now fill me with Your Holy Spirit and guide me into all truth (John 16:13). In Jesus' name, I pray. Amen."

Battle Command over Homes, Cities, and Nations

- "Satan, I (we) come against you in the name of the Lord Jesus Christ. I (we) am (are) armed with the blood (Rev.12:11) and the Word of God, my (our) sword (Eph.6:17). Right now, I (we) pierce you through with the truth that Jesus Christ came in the flesh to destroy your works (1 John 3:8).

- "Even now, as I (we) lift my (our) praises to the Lord, the chief prince (Dan. 10:13) assigned to rule over this home, ministry, city, etc., has been bound with fetters of iron (Ps. 149:8). I (we) break the assignment of the world ruler over this (home, ministry, city, etc.), in the name of Jesus. Satan, you are also bound with chains of iron.

- "Whatever I (we) bind on earth is bound in heaven (Matt. 18:18), and with that authority I (we) cast you down. By faith I (we) scatter every heavenly force arrayed against me (us) as holy angels smite them on my (our) behalf (2 Kings 19:35).

- "Greater is He that is in me (us) and more powerful are those with me (us) than those with you (1 John 4:4). Jesus Christ Himself sends His Word to deliver me (us) from your devices.

- "I (we) put to flight every demonic power in this (home, ministry, city, etc.) that would hinder the work and Word of God from going forth in this place. Satan, I (we) have bound your chiefs; therefore, all your demons grope in darkness, staggering as I (we) smite them by the resurrection power of Jesus.

- I (we) laugh and God laughs (Ps. 2:4) as I (we) see you brought to derision as you recognize that you must bow at the name of Jesus (Phil. 2:10). Jesus is Lord over these homes, ministries, cities, countries, etc.

- Now by faith I (we) loose the peace and grace and truth of Christ. Come, Holy Spirit, and do Your good work here, saving, healing, delivering, as I (we) see

Your kingdom established (Rev. 11:15) to the glory of the Father. Amen."

Shattering Strongholds

- "In the name of Jesus, I bind my body, soul, and spirit to the will and purposes of my God. I bind myself to an awareness of the power of the blood of Jesus working in my life every day. I bind my mind to the mind of Christ that I may have the thoughts, purposes, and feelings of His heart in me. I bind my feet to the paths You have ordained for me to walk in, Lord, so that my steps will be strong and steady. I bind myself to the work of the cross with all of its mercy, truth, love, power, forgiveness, and dying to self. In Jesus' name, amen."
- "In the name of Jesus, I bind the strongman and loose his hold on everything he has ever stolen from me (health, wealth, peace, family, etc.). I rebuke his works and loose the power and effects of every deception, device, and influence he wants to bring against me. In Jesus' name, amen."
- "Lord, I repent of having wrong attitudes and thoughts. I renounce them now and ask Your forgiveness. I loose every old wrong pattern of thinking, attitude, idea, desire, belief, habit, and behavior that may still be working in me. I tear down, crush, smash, and destroy every stronghold I have erected to protect these wrong attitudes. I bind myself to the attitudes and patterns of Jesus Christ. I bind myself to the overcoming behavior and spiritual desires that line up with the fruit of the Holy Spirit. In Jesus' name, amen."

- "Father, I loose any stronghold in my life protecting wrong feelings I have against anyone. Forgive me as I forgive those who have caused me pain, loss, or grief. I loose any desire for retribution or rectification. In the name of Jesus, I loose the power and effects of any harsh or hard words (word curses) spoken about me, to me, or by me. I loose any strongholds connected with them. I loose all generational bondages and their strongholds from me. I thank You, Jesus, that You have promised that whatsoever I bind and loose on earth will be bound and loosed in heaven. In Jesus' name, amen."

- "Father, in the name of Jesus, I bind myself, soul and spirit, to Your will and purposes. I bind myself to the truth, to a fresh awareness of the blood, to the mind of Christ, and to the work of the cross. I loose and shatter every hindrance and device that my soul would use to distract me from moving deeper in You. I loose, shatter, and destroy every wrong agreement I have ever entered into, whether it was with another person, a wrong spirit, a deception, or a false philosophy. I loose, sever, and cut myself from all soul ties I have ever formed with anyone. I loose, sever, and destroy any justifications, logic, arguments, or reasoning that I have ever held on to in order to excuse wrong attitudes, wrong patterns, wrong behavior, or unforgiveness in my life. In Jesus' name, amen."

- "I loose the grave clothes from my soul. I loose any generational bondage from my soul. I loose any opposition and resistance from my soul, and I loose any hidden agendas from my soul. I loose, shatter, and destroy the layer of self-control and self-defense that I have allowed my soul to put down over my unmet needs, my unhealed hurts, and my unresolved issues. Father, some of them have been there for so long, and I have believed they would never be fixed. Forgive me, Father, for believing this; help me to work with You to loose layer after layer so that these layers of vulnerability can be exposed to Your healing grace.

- Thank You for helping me to continue to loose and destroy every fear that I will be disappointed and hurt if my unmet needs come to the surface of my soul. I loose and shatter every wrong belief I have ever had, that You wouldn't fix every single lock and wrong in my life and that You wouldn't make me whole and strong and filled with joy. In Jesus' name, amen.

- "Father, I ask You to forgive me my doubts and to cleanse me and guide my steps towards becoming the fulfillment of Your purpose for me from my birth. I thank You, Father, because I know it is Your will to do this for me. In Jesus' name, amen."

Prayer for Your Children

- "I thank You, Father, for the gift of my children that You have given me. I bring them before Your throne of grace and mercy, thanking You that You will perfect that which concerns me (Ps. 138:8).

- "I thank You, Father, that You formed them in my womb, that you planned for their birth (Jer. 1:5), and that from the moment of conception, they have been alive in You.

128

- "Thank You, Father, that You have lifted (names of children) above those that rise up against them (Ps. 18:45), that You deliver them from the evil man and preserve them from the violent man (Ps. 140:1).
- "Thank You that You keep (names) from any trap that has been laid for them, and that the wicked will fall together into their own nets, while You pass over my children and help them escape. In Jesus' name, amen."

Prayer for Parents

- "Thank You, Father, for Your wisdom, revelation, and understanding upon us as parents to lead and direct (names of children) into Your paths of righteousness that they might dwell in the secret place of the Most High. Because (names) have made You their refuge and their dwelling place, there shall no evil befall them, for You give Your angels charge over (names) to accompany and defend them in all their ways (Ps. 91:1, 9–11).
- Thank you, Father, that (names) do not love or cherish the world or the things that are in the world, but that they are eager to do Your will and carry out Your purpose in their lives. (Names) keep in their hearts what they have heard from the first, and (names) will dwell in the Son and in You, Father (1 John 2:15, 17, 24).
- "Thank You, Father, that (names) abide in You, are rooted in You, are knit to You, and that (names) abide in Christ so that when He is made visible, they will not shrink from His coming (1 John 2:28).

- "Then God's peace will be theirs, that tranquil state of a soul assured of its salvation through Christ. They will fear nothing from God and be content with their earthly lot, and that peace that transcends all understanding shall garrison and mount guard over their hearts and minds in Christ Jesus (Phil 4:7). In Jesus' name, amen."

Confessions

Great faith is the product of great fights. Great testimonies are the outcome of great tests. Great triumphs come only out of great trials. Every stumbling block must become a stepping stone, and every opposition must become an opportunity.

—Smith Wigglesworth

- "Although my day may be filled with darkness and confusion, I speak light. The Lord and His Word are my light and my salvation; whom then shall I fear?
- "I have ears to hear; therefore, I will hear God's instruction today. God's Word will be a lamp to my feet and a light to my path. His promises are a light into my life today.
- "God's Word will give me guidance. God's Word shows me what to do. The Holy Spirit has been sent to show me things to come. The Holy Spirit will also be a light in my life today, because I am a mature child of God.
- "I am in covenant with God, bought by the blood of Jesus. The blood of Jesus covers me. I am led by the Holy Spirit. The Holy Spirit shows me what to do. Angels watch over me and protect me.

- "They will keep me from dashing my foot against a stone. No problem is bigger than the Word of God. No problem is bigger than the Holy Spirit. No problem is bigger than my angels. Therefore, no problem is bigger than me. God will arise in me.
- "My enemies will be scattered. If God be for me, who can be against me? I am God's sheep. I know His voice. I will not follow a stranger. I am righteous. I walk in God's ways. Therefore, my path grows brighter every day.
- "I am walking away from the darkness, away from the confusion and into the light of God's will. Today will be a good day. It's another day the Lord has made for me to rejoice in and be glad about. God is leading me. Goodness and mercy are following me.
- "Because God loves me, when I lie down tonight, God will give me sleep. This will be a good day because I cannot fail! In Jesus' name, amen.
- "Lord, I lift up my eyes this day toward You. Jesus, grace, truth, and compassion are brought to life in You.
- "Thank You for Your grace in me and that the truth of Your message will change my life and compel me in unrelenting love to You, Lord.
- "The ministry that comes from You, Jesus, back toward me, I will release in ministry toward all in need. In Jesus' name, amen."

An Overcomer's Confession

- "My body is the temple of the Holy Spirit, redeemed, cleansed, and sanctified by the blood of Jesus.

- "My members, the parts of my body, are instruments of righteousness, yielded to God for His service and for His glory. The devil has no place in me, no power over me, and no unsettled claims against me.
- "All has been settled by the blood of Jesus. I overcome Satan by the blood of the Lamb and the word of my testimony, and I love not my life unto death. My body is for the Lord, and the Lord is for my body. In Jesus' name, amen."

Committing to Jesus

- "Lord Jesus, I commit my life to You totally, spirit, soul, and body. I ask that You bend, break, and mold me into the person that You want me to be. Lord, teach me to trust in You and to live and walk by faith in You and Your Word.
- "I commit to You, Lord, to take accountability and responsibility in my walk with You and Your Word. No more will the enemy's devices and the deceptions of the old man easily sway me.
- "I purpose today to firmly and totally fix my eyes and heart on You, Lord. I press, push, and apprehend all that You have for me today, keeping in the back of my remembrance that the enemy loves a lazy or slothful mind.
- "Satan, I come against you and all hosts of hell, and I reject everything that you would have for me today. Satan, I refuse all snares, pits, and traps that you have set to draw me away from my Lord Jesus Christ.
- "I rebuke you, Satan, and all your hosts, in the name of Jesus, from every assignment you have assigned

against me or my family, my property, my health, and my finances.

- "Father, I ask and believe for Your best in my life today and that Your will and purposes will be done in and through me. I also ask that You keep me in Your perfect will and make me a yielded vessel fit for Your work today.
- "I place myself under the shadow of the Almighty. I will say of the Lord, 'He is my refuge and my fortress; My God, in Him I will trust,' for I choose to dwell in the secret place of the Most High. In Jesus' name, amen."

A Confession for Healing

- "Father, I believe Jesus Christ Himself took my diseases and my sicknesses on the cross.
- "I believe that with His stripes that He took in His body, I am healed. I am the healed. I receive Jesus as my personal healer, just as I have received Him as my Lord and Savior.
- "The power to resist sickness lives inside of me. I thank You for the gift of the body of your Son, Jesus Christ. Amen."

Answers for Your Prayers from God the Father

Father's Love Letter

This letter is the answer to your prayers from your Father, who art in heaven; who is your Lord and personal Savior, Jesus Christ, who died on Calvary's cross just for you; and the Holy Spirit, who is your Comforter.

A letter to My child:

- **You may not know me, but I know everything about you.** Psalm 139:1: *"O LORD, you have searched me [thoroughly] and have known me."*
- **I know when you sit down and when you rise up.** Psalm 139:2: *"You know my downsitting and my uprising; you understand my thought afar off."*
- **I am familiar with all your ways.** Psalm 139:3: *"You sift and search out my path and my lying down, and you are acquainted with all my ways."*
- **Even the very hairs on your head are numbered.** Matthew 10:29–31: *"Are not two little sparrows sold for a penny? And yet not one of them will fall to the ground without your Father's leave (consent)*

and notice. But even the very hairs of your head are all numbered. Fear not, then; you are of more value than many sparrows."

- **For you were made in My image.** Genesis 1:27: *"So God created man in His own image, in the image and likeness of God He created him; male and female He created them."*
- **In Me you live and move and have your being.** Acts 17:28: *"For in Him we live and move and have our being; as even some of your [own] poets have said, for we are also His offspring."*
- **For you are my offspring.** Acts 17:28: *"For in Him we live and move and have our being; as even some of your [own] poets have said, for we are also His offspring."*
- **I knew you even before you were conceived.** Jeremiah 1:4–5: *"Before I formed you in the womb I knew [and] approved of you [as my chosen instrument], and before you were born, I separated and set you apart, consecrating you; [and] I appointed you as a prophet to the nations."*
- **I chose you when I planned creation.** Ephesians 1:11–12: *"In Him we also were made [God's] heritage (portion) and we obtained an inheritance; for we had been foreordained (chosen and appointed beforehand) in accordance with His purpose, Who works out everything in agreement with the counsel and design of His [own] will, so that we who first hoped in Christ [who first put our confidence in Him have been destined and appointed to] live for the praise of His glory!"*
- **You were not a mistake, for all your days are written in My book.** Psalm 139:15–16: *"My frame*

was not hidden from You when I was being formed in secret [and] intricately and curiously wrought [as if embroidered with various colors] in the depths of the earth [a region of darkness and mystery]. Your eyes saw my unformed substance, and in your book all the days [of my life] were written before ever they took shape, when as yet there was none of them."

- **I determined the exact time of your birth and where you would live.** Acts 17:26: *"And He made from one [common origin, one source, one blood] all nations of men to settle on the face of the earth, having definitely determined [their] allotted periods of time and the fixed boundaries of their habitation (their settlements, lands, and abodes)."*

- **You are fearfully and wonderfully made.** Psalm 139:14: *"I will confess and praise You for You are fearful and wonderful and for the awful wonder of my birth! Wonderful are your works, and that my inner self knows right well."*

- **I knit you together in your mother's womb.** Psalm 139:13: *"For You did form my inward parts; You did knit me together in my mother's womb."*

- **And brought you forth on the day you were born.** Psalm 71:6: *"Upon You have I leaned and relied from birth; You are He who took me from my mother's womb and You have been my benefactor from that day. My praise is continually of You."*

- **I have been misrepresented by those who don't know me.** John 8:41–44: *"You are doing the works of your [own] father. They said to Him, We are not illegitimate children and born out of fornication; we have one Father, even God. Jesus said to them, If God were your Father, you would love Me and* *respect Me and welcome Me gladly, for I proceeded (came forth) from God [out of His very presence]. I did not even come on My own authority or of My own accord (as self-appointed); but He sent Me. Why do you misunderstand what I say? It is because you are unable to hear what I am saying. [You cannot bear to listen to my message; your ears are shut to my teaching.] You are of your father, the devil, and it is your will to practice the lusts and gratify the desires [which are characteristic] of your father. He was a murderer from the beginning and does not stand in the truth, because there is no truth in him. When he speaks a falsehood, he speaks what is natural to him, for he is a liar [himself] and the father of lies and of all that is false."*

- **I am not distant and angry, but am the complete expression of love.** John 4:16: *"At this, Jesus said to her, Go, call your husband and come back here."*
- **And it is My desire to lavish My love on you.** 1 John 3:1: *"See what an incredible] quality of love the Father has given (shown, bestowed on) us, that we should [be permitted to] be named and called and counted the children of God! And so we are! The reason that the world does not know (recognize, acknowledge) us is that it does not know (recognize, acknowledge) Him."*
- **Simply because you are My child and I am your father.** 1 John 3:1: *" "See what an incredible] quality of love the Father has given (shown, bestowed on) us, that we should [be permitted to] be named and called and counted the children of God! And so we are! The reason that the world does not know*

138

(recognize, acknowledge) us is that it does not know (recognize, acknowledge) Him."

- **I offer you more than your earthly father ever could.** Matthew 7:11: "If you then, evil as you are, know how to give good and advantageous gifts to your children, how much more will your Father Who is in heaven [perfect as He is] give good and advantageous things to those who keep on asking Him!"

- **For I am the perfect father.** Matthew 5:48: *"You, therefore, must be perfect [growing into complete maturity of godliness in mind and character, having reached the proper height of virtue and integrity], as your heavenly Father is perfect."*

- **Every good gift that you receive comes from My hand.** James 1:17: *"Every good gift and every perfect (free, large, full) gift is from above; it comes down from the Father of all [that gives] light, in [the shining of] Whom there can be no variation [rising or setting] or shadow cast by His turning [as in an eclipse]."*

- **For I am your provider, and I meet all your needs.** Matthew 6:31–33: *"Therefore do not worry and be anxious, saying, what are we going to have to eat? Or, what are we going to have to drink? Or, what are we going to have to wear? For the Gentiles (heathen) wish for and crave and diligently seek all these things, and your heavenly Father knows well that you need them all. But seek (aim at and strive after) first of all His kingdom and His righteousness (His way of doing and being right), and then all these things taken together will be given you besides."*

- **My plan for your future has always been filled with hope.** Jeremiah 29:11: *"For I know the thoughts and plans that I have for you, says the Lord, thoughts and plans for welfare and peace and not for evil, to give you hope in your final outcome."*
- **Because I love you with an everlasting love.** Jeremiah 31:3: *"The Lord appeared from of old to me [Israel], saying, Yes, I have loved you with an everlasting love; therefore with loving-kindness have I drawn you and continued my faithfulness to you."*
- **My thoughts toward you are as countless as the sand on the seashore.** Psalm 139:17–18: *"How precious and weighty also are your thoughts to me, O God! How vast is the sum of them! If I could count them, they would be more in number than the sand. When I awoke [could I count to the end], I would still be with You."*
- **And I rejoice over you with singing.** Zephaniah 3:17: *"The Lord your God is in the midst of you, a Mighty One, a Savior [Who saves]! He will rejoice over you with joy; He will rest [in silent satisfaction] and in His love He will be silent and make no mention [of past sins, or even recall them]; He will exult over you with singing."*
- **I will never stop doing good to you.** Jeremiah 32:40: *"And I will make an everlasting covenant with them: I will not turn away from following them to do them good, and I will put My [reverential] fear in their hearts, so that they will not depart from Me."*
- **For you are my treasured possession.** Exodus 19:5: *"Now therefore, if you will obey My voice in*

truth and keep My covenant, then you shall be My own peculiar possession and treasure from among and above all people; for all the earth is Mine."

- **I desire to establish you with all My heart and all My soul.** Jeremiah 32:41: *"Yes, I will rejoice over them to do them good, and I will plant them in this land assuredly and in truth with My whole heart and with My whole being."*

- **And I want to show you great and marvelous things.** Jeremiah 33:3: *"'Call to me and I will answer you and tell you great and unsearchable things you do not know."*

- **If you seek Me with all your heart, you will find Me.** Deuteronomy 4:29: *"But if from there you will seek (inquire for and require as necessity) the Lord your God, you will find Him if you [truly] seek Him with all your heart [and mind] and soul and life."*

- **Delight in Me and I will give you the desires of your heart.** Psalm 37:4: *"Delight yourself also in the Lord, and He will give you the desires and secret petitions of your heart."*

- **For it is I who gave you those desires.** Philippians 2:13: *"[Not in your own strength] for it is God who is all the while effectually at work in you [energizing and creating in you the power and desire], both to will and to work for His good pleasure and satisfaction and delight."*

- **I am able to do more for you than you could possibly imagine.** Ephesians 3:20: *"Now to Him Who, by (in consequence of) the [action of His] power that is at work within us, is able to [carry out His purpose and] do superabundantly, far over and above all that we [dare] ask or think [infinitely* *beyond our highest prayers, desires, thoughts, hopes, or dreams]."*

- **For I am your greatest encourager.** 2 Thessalonians 2:16–17: *"Now may our Lord Jesus Christ Himself and God our Father, Who loved us and gave us everlasting consolation and encouragement and well-founded hope through [His] grace (unmerited favor), comfort and encourage your hearts and strengthen them [make them steadfast and keep them unswerving] in every good work and word."*

- **I am also the Father who comforts you in all your troubles.** 2 Corinthians 1:3–4: *"Blessed be the God and Father of our Lord Jesus Christ, the Father of sympathy (pity and mercy) and the God [Who is the Source] of every comfort (consolation and encouragement), Who comforts (consoles and encourages) us in every trouble (calamity and affliction), so that we may also be able to comfort (console and encourage) those who are in any kind of trouble or distress, with the comfort (consolation and encouragement) with which we ourselves are comforted (consoled and encouraged) by God."*

- **When you are brokenhearted, I am close to you.** Psalm 34:18: *"The Lord is close to those who are of a broken heart and saves such as are crushed with sorrow for sin and are humbly and thoroughly penitent."*

- **As a shepherd carries a lamb, I have carried you close to My heart.** Isaiah 40:11: *"He will feed His flock like a shepherd: He will gather the lambs in His arm, He will carry them in His bosom and will gently lead those that have their young."*

- **One day I will wipe away every tear from your eyes.** Revelation 21:3–4: *"Then I heard a mighty voice from the throne and I perceived its distinct words, saying, See! The abode of God is with men, and He will live (encamp, tent) among them; and they shall be His people, and God shall personally be with them and be their God."*

- **And I'll take away all the pain you have suffered on this earth.** Revelation 21:3–4: *"Then I heard a mighty voice from the throne and I perceived its distinct words, saying, See! The abode of God is with men, and He will live (encamp, tent) among them; and they shall be His people, and God shall personally be with them and be their God."*

- **I am your Father, and I love you even as I love My son, Jesus.** John 17:23: *"I in them and You in Me, in order that they may become one and perfectly united, that the world may know and [definitely] recognize that You sent Me and that You have loved them [even] as You have loved Me."*

- **For in Jesus, My love for you is revealed.** John 17:26: *"I have made Your Name known to them and revealed Your character and Your very Self, and I will continue to make [You] known, that the love which You have bestowed upon Me may be in them [felt in their hearts] and that I [Myself] may be in them."*

- **He is the exact representation of my being.** Hebrews 1:3: *"He is the sole expression of the glory of God [the Light-being, the out-raying or radiance of the divine], and He is the perfect imprint and very image of [God's] nature, upholding and maintaining and guiding and propelling the universe by*

His mighty word of power. When He had by offering Himself accomplished our cleansing of sins and riddance of guilt, He sat down at the right hand of the divine Majesty on high."

- **He came to demonstrate that I am for you, not against you.** Romans 8:31: *"What then shall we say to [all] this? If God is for us, who [can be] against us? [Who can be our foe, if God is on our side?]."*

- **And to tell you that I am not counting your sins.** 2 Corinthians 5:18–19: *"But all things are from God, Who through Jesus Christ reconciled us to Himself [received us into favor, brought us into harmony with Himself] and gave to us the ministry of reconciliation [that by word and deed we might aim to bring others into harmony with Him]. It was God [personally present] in Christ, reconciling and restoring the world to favor with Himself, not counting up and holding against [men] their trespasses [but canceling them], and committing to us the message of reconciliation (of the restoration to favor)."*

- **Jesus died so that you and all people could be reconciled.** 2 Corinthians 5:18–19: *"But all things are from God, Who through Jesus Christ reconciled us to Himself [received us into favor, brought us into harmony with Himself] and gave to us the ministry of reconciliation [that by word and deed we might aim to bring others into harmony with Him]. It was God [personally present] in Christ, reconciling and restoring the world to favor with Himself, not counting up and holding against [men] their trespasses [but canceling them], and committing to us* the message of reconciliation (of the restoration to favor)."

- **His death was the ultimate expression of My love for you.** 1 John 4:10: *"In this is love: not that we loved God, but that He loved us and sent His Son to be the propitiation (the atoning sacrifice) for our sins."*

- **I gave up everything I loved that I might gain your love.** Romans 8:31–32: *"What then shall we say to [all] this? If God is for us, who [can be] against us? [Who can be our foe, if God is on our side?] He who did not withhold or spare [even] His own Son but gave Him up for us all, will He not also with Him freely and graciously give us all [other] things?"*

- **If you receive the gift of My Son, Jesus, you receive Me.** 1 John 2:23: *"No one who [habitually] denies (disowns) the Son even has the Father. Whoever confesses (acknowledges and has) the Son has the Father also."*

- **And nothing will ever separate you from My love again.** Romans 8:38–39: *"For I am persuaded beyond doubt (am sure) that neither death nor life, nor angels nor principalities, nor things impending and threatening, nor things to come, nor powers, nor height nor depth, nor anything else in all creation will be able to separate us from the love of God which is in Christ Jesus our Lord."*

- **Come home and I'll throw the biggest party heaven has ever seen.** Luke 15:7: *"Thus, I tell you, there will be more joy in heaven over one [especially] wicked person who repents (changes his mind, abhorring his errors and misdeeds, and deter-*

mines to enter upon a better course of life) than over ninety-nine righteous persons who have no need of repentance."

- **I have always been Father and will always be Father.** Ephesians 3:14–15: *"For this reason [seeing the greatness of this plan by which you are built together in Christ], I bow my knees before the Father of our Lord Jesus Christ, for Whom every family in heaven and on earth is named [that Father from Whom all fatherhood takes its title and derives its name]."*

- **My question is, Will you be My child?** John 1:12–13: *"But to as many as did receive and welcome Him, He gave the authority (power, privilege, right) to become the children of God, that is, to those who believe in (adhere to, trust in, and rely on) His name. Who owe their birth neither to bloods nor to the will of the flesh [that of physical impulse] nor to the will of man [that of a natural father], but to God. [They are born of God!]."*

- **I am waiting for you.** Luke 15:11–32: *"And He said, There was a certain man who had two sons; and the younger of them said to his father, Father, give me the part of the property that falls [to me]. And he divided the estate between them. And not many days after that, the younger son gathered up all that he had and journeyed into a distant country, and there he wasted his fortune in reckless and loose [from restraint] living. And when he had spent all he had, a mighty famine came upon that country, and he began to fall behind and be in want. So he went and forced (glued) himself upon one of the citizens of that country, who sent him into his fields to feed* *hogs. And he would gladly have fed on and filled his belly with the carob pods that the hogs were eating, but [they could not satisfy his hunger and] nobody gave him anything [better]. Then when he came to himself, he said, How many hired servants of my father have enough food, and [even food] to spare, but I am perishing (dying) here of hunger! I will get up and go to my father, and I will say to him, Father, I have sinned against heaven and in your sight. I am no longer worthy to be called your son; [just] make me like one of your hired servants. So he got up and came to his [own] father. But while he was still a long way off, his father saw him and was moved with pity and tenderness [for him]; and he ran and embraced him and kissed him [fervently]. And the son said to him, Father, I have sinned against heaven and in your sight; I am no longer worthy to be called your son [I no longer deserve to be recognized as a son of yours]! But the father said to his bond servants, Bring quickly the best robe (the festive robe of honor) and put it on him; and give him a ring for his hand and sandals for his feet. And bring out that [wheat-]fattened calf and kill it; and let us revel and feast and be happy and make merry, Because this my son was dead and is alive again; he was lost and is found! And they began to revel and feast and make merry. But his older son was in the field; and as he returned and came near the house, he heard music and dancing. And having called one of the servant [boys] to him, he began to ask what this meant. And he said to him, Your brother has come, and your father has killed that [wheat-]fattened calf, because he has received him back safe and well. But [the*

147

elder brother] was angry [with deep-seated wrath] and resolved not to go in. Then his father came out and began to plead with him, but he answered his father, Look! These many years I have served you, and I have never disobeyed your command. Yet you never gave me [so much as] a [little] kid, that I might revel and feast and be happy and make merry with my friends; but when this son of yours arrived, who has devoured your estate with immoral women, you have killed for him that [wheat-] fattened calf! And the father said to him, Son, you are always with me, and all that is mine is yours. But it was fitting to make merry, to revel and feast and rejoice, for this brother of yours was dead and is alive again! He was lost and is found!"

Love,

Your Dad, almighty God

Allow Him Today to Be Your Savior and Lord

This righteousness from God comes through faith in Jesus Christ to all who believe. There is no difference, for all have sinned and fall short of the glory of God, and are justified freely by his grace through the redemption that came by Christ Jesus."

—Romans 3:22–24

God is indeed a God who answers prayers. He is a loving God, and He knows your need. Keep trusting in Him. The Bible says the steps of a righteous man are ordered by the Lord. And if you don't know Him as Lord and Savior, then look below and read the "Plan of Salvation." Then read the next chapter, "A Message of Hope."

He is a loving God and is waiting to deliver you from the hands of the enemy. No matter what has happened to you in life, He still loves you. It doesn't matter what sin you have committed—He still loves you and is waiting on you to come to Him. When the world forsakes you, He will never forsake you. His Word declares that He will never leave you nor forsake you, even to the very end. God loves you, and if you would like to enjoy the benefits of

His healing and delivering power, then accept Him as Lord and Savior or renew your commitment to Him today.

How to Receive Power and Authority Through the Miracle of Salvation

Plan of Salvation

If you have read this book and would like to enjoy the benefit of God's blessings in healing, deliverance, break-throughs, and freedom from evil forces, then you need to know Jesus Christ as Lord and Savior. If you don't know Jesus Christ as your personal Lord and Savior, then read the plan of salvation explained below. If you once knew the Lord Jesus Christ as your Lord and Savior but back-slid, then pray the prayer of faith for your miracle of salvation to be restored.

One of the greatest miracles is the miracle of salvation. The Bible says the whole of heaven rejoices when one soul comes to repentance. If ever you're going to receive that deliverance that you are believing God for, you must accept the deliverer—and His name is Jesus Christ. The Bible also says that believe and you shall receive.

First: The Bible declares, "I am come that they might have life, and that they might have it more abundantly" (John 10:10). Giving you abundant life required the supreme sacrifice: "For God so loved the world that he gave his only begotten Son, that whosoever believeth in him should not perish, but have everlasting life" (John 3:16). God desires fellowship and companionship with you. What a wonderful gift the Father has given; yet if God gave His own Son to provide an abundant and everlasting life, why don't more people have what He has designed for them to receive? It is a question answered by a sobering realization.

Second: There is a gap between God and mankind. He has provided a way for us to receive an abundant and eternal life, but people throughout the ages have made selfish choices to disobey God almighty. These choices continue to cause separation from the Father. God's Word shows us that the result of sin is death. God says in His Word, "There is a way which seemeth right unto a man, but the ends thereof are the ways of death" (Prov. 14:12). And God also said, "But your iniquities have separated between you and your God, and sins have hid his face from you, that he will not hear" (Isa. 59:2). Paul the apostle states in Romans 3:23, "For the wages of sin is death; but the gift of God is eternal life through Jesus Christ our Lord." Every human was created with the ability and need to know God and fellowship with Him. Augustine, a minister who lived during the fourth and fifth centuries, called this longing in each of us "that God-shaped vacuum." Every day we hear of people who are rich, famous, achievers, star athletes — people who seem to have the best that life can offer — yet they try to fill that empty void in their lives with things. They even try good works, morality, and religion. Yet they remain empty, for only God, through His Son, can fill that emptiness.

Third: Jesus Christ, God's Son, is the only way to God. Only He can reconcile us to God the Father. Mankind may seek other solutions and worship other gods, but Jesus Christ alone died on the cross for our sins and rose in triumph over the grave and eternal death. He paid the penalty for our sin and bridged the gap between God and mankind. The Bible explains, "But God commendeth his love toward us, in that, while we were yet sinners, Christ died for us" (Rom. 5:8). We are also told, "For Christ also hath once suffered for sins, the just for the unjust, that he might bring us to God" (1 Pet. 3:18). There is only one way provided: "For there is one God and one mediator between God and men, the man Christ Jesus" (1 Tim. 2:5). For in John 14:6, we read, "Jesus saith unto him, I am the way, the truth, and the life: no man cometh unto the Father, but by me." God almighty has provided the only way. Jesus Christ paid the penalty for our sin and rebellion against God by dying on the cross, shedding His blood, and rising from the dead to justify and reconcile us back to God the Father.

Fourth: You can be brought back to God, and your relationship with Him can be restored by trusting in Christ alone to save your life from destruction. What an incredible exchange: your worst for God's best! This step happens by asking Jesus Christ to take away your sin and to come into your heart to be your Lord and Savior. God's Word is very clear: "Behold, I stand at the door, and knock: if any man hear my voice, and open the door, I will come in to him, and will sup with him, and he with me" (Rev. 3:20). And the Bible tells us, "That if thou shalt confess with thy mouth the Lord Jesus, and shalt believe in thine heart that God hath raised him from the dead, thou shalt be saved" (Rom. 10:9). Are you willing to let go of your burdens and sins? Are you willing to turn away from and repent of your sins? Are you willing to receive Jesus Christ as your Lord and Savior now?

Fifth: At this moment, you can pray the most important prayer of your life by simply saying:

Dear Lord Jesus,

I believe You are the Son of God. I believe You came to earth two thousand years ago. I believe You died for me on the cross and shed Your blood for my salvation. I believe You rose from the dead and ascended on high. I believe You are coming back again to earth. Dear Jesus, I am a sinner. Forgive my sins. Cleanse me now with Your precious blood. Come into my heart. Save my soul right now. I give you my life. I receive You now as my Savior, my Lord, and my God. I am Yours forever, and I will serve You and follow You the rest of my days. From this moment on, I belong to You only. I no longer belong to this world or to the enemy of my soul. I belong to You; I am born again. Amen!

By your praying this prayer, confessing your sins, and receiving Jesus Christ into your heart, God has given you the right to become His forgiven child. The Bible gives you this assurance: "But as many as received him, to them he gave the power to become the sons of God, even to them who believe on his name" (John1:12).

A Message of Hope

Knowing Jesus as Lord and Savior

If you don't know Jesus Christ as your personal Lord and Savior, then these militant warfare prayers can't work for you. It is for those who believe in Him and serve Him daily. But you can have the opportunity today to receive Him as your personal Lord and Savior. If you would like to receive power and authority from Jesus Christ to destroy the work of the devil over your life, then accept Him today as your Lord and Savior.

Jesus has given power and authority to all those who believe in Him. The Bible says that Jesus Christ gives to every believer power and authority over the enemy. He gives healing to those who believe in Him and sets free those who know him as Lord and Savior, because He is a loving God.

God Is Love

The Bible says that God is love—pure love. And He wants to lavish His love on you. He is not looking for more servants to add to His kingdom, but more children to fill His house. He wants to be in relationship with you, not because you deserve it, but just because He made you and is head over heels in love with you.

God's Original Intent

It was God's original plan in the Garden of Eden that Adam and Eve would live all the days of their lives in the presence of a loving Father and would in turn reflect His love to their children. It was the Father's hope that each generation would grow up in the light of His love, never knowing a day of rejection or pain.

Love Cannot Be Forced

However, love is not something that can be forced, so God gave Adam and Eve the privilege of a free will. They had the freedom to trust God and stay in the garden or disobey Him and leave. In Genesis we read that the latter happened, and as a result of their choice to become independent, they became separated from God.

Broken Relationships

As a result of Adam and Eve's actions, a new deadly disease called "sin" infected humanity. The world that God originally intended to be perfect and full of love was now wrought with pain and suffering because of the consequences of sin. Hurting people tend to hurt others, which is a legacy that has been passed on from generation to generation.

Understanding Our Need for Love

Since God created us for love, we are born with a great expectation to be loved and accepted. It is a scientific fact that babies who are not shown loving touch in the first few months of their lives can be physically and emotionally affected for the rest of their lives.

We All Have a Love Deficit

Unfortunately, our parents could express only the love that they first received from their parents. As a result, many of us have grown up with love deficits in our hearts. While we may know we are missing something, we might not be able to identify the emptiness that resides in the deepest parts of our beings.

Filling the Void

All we know is that we need to try and fill the emptiness somehow. Some try to fill this void in relationships, others in performance and success. And others seek to dull the emptiness with addictions. No matter what we do, if we do not encounter the real thing, we will always be left with a feeling of emptiness and unfulfillment.

Having a Personal Relationship with God

There is only one place where we will find the true love and acceptance that we are looking for, and that is in a personal relationship with God. We were all born with a God sized "hole in our soul" that can be filled only by God Himself. Many of us have tried to fill this void with other things, but it is like putting a square peg in a round hole. It just doesn't fit.

The Good News

The good news is that God wants to be in a relationship with us more than we want to be in a relationship with Him. The one who knew us before we were conceived (Jer. 1:4) and who knit us together in our mothers' wombs

(Ps. 139:13) wants to be our Father. Though we are His offspring by creation, His desire is that we might become His children through redemption.

Finding Our Way Home

While we were still estranged, God the Father made a way for us to come home by sending His only Son, Jesus Christ, to earth two thousand years ago to take care of the sin issue that had kept us separated from Him. In obedience to His Father, Jesus bore upon Himself the weight of our sin, nailing it to the cross so that we could be born into His wonderful family.

Jesus Is the Way to the Father

His resurrection from the dead signaled the victory that would allow many sons and daughters to come into glory! In John 14:6, Jesus says, "I am the way, the truth, and the life; no man comes to the Father except through me." Our access to the Father is through Jesus alone. His sacrifice was the one and only price that could be paid for our redemption and restoration into the family of His wonderful Father. If we receive God's gift of His Son, Jesus Christ, we receive the right to become children of God!

Would You Like to Receive This Gift?

If you would like to accept this gift (eternal life in relationship with God), Jesus Christ has secured it for you. All you need to do is to tell God that you want to be saved. You are saved by believing, and the words below might help you express your thoughts to God. It's not these exact words that will save you, but the attitude of your heart towards God.

A Prayer to Accept or Reaffirm Your Relationship with Jesus Christ

Father, I'm coming home. Please make me Your child. I turn from my sin. I accept Your forgiveness made possible through Jesus Christ by His death and resurrection. I place my faith and trust in Jesus alone. I receive Him as my Savior and Lord. I want to follow and serve You. Let today be the beginning of my new journey as Your child and a member of Your family. Thank You for making a way for me to come home. In Jesus' name, I pray. Amen.

Your New Relationship with God

As you begin your new life as God's child, you will have the privilege of getting to know Him as your Father. You are now part of His incredible family! By faith in Jesus Christ, you can be assured of the following truths.

1. **You are God's child (John 1:12–13).**
   "Yet to all who received him, to those who believed in his name, he gave the right to become children of God—children born not of natural descent, nor of human decision or a husband's will, but born of God" (NIV).

2. **God loves you (1 John 3:1).**
   "How great is the love the Father has lavished on us, that we should be called the children of God! And that is what we are!" (NIV).

3. **You have the assurance of eternal life (John 3:16).**

"For God so loved the world, that he gave his one and only Son, that whoever believes in him shall not perish but have eternal life" (NIV).

4. **He put His Holy Spirit in you (2 Cor. 1:21–22).**

"Now it is God who makes both us and you stand firm in Christ. He anointed us, set his seal of ownership on us, and put his Spirit in our hearts as a deposit guaranteeing what is to come."

5. **You can talk directly to God (Matt. 7:7–11).**

"Ask and it will be given to you; seek and you will find; knock and the door will be opened to you. For everyone who asks receives; he who seeks finds, and to him who knocks, the door will be opened. Which of you, if his son asks for bread, will give him a stone? Or if he asks for a fish, will give him a snake? If you, then, though you are evil, know how to give good gifts to your children, how much more will your Father in heaven give good gifts to those who ask him!" (NIV).

6. **Nothing will ever separate you from His love (Rom. 8:38).**

"For I am convinced that neither death nor life, neither angels nor demons, neither the present nor the future, nor any powers, neither height nor depth, nor anything in all creation, will be able to separate us from the love of God that is in Christ Jesus our Lord."

Steps to Help You in Your Walk with God

Follow these basic steps to help you in your walk with God, because you are now a born- again Christian.

1. Get a Bible and read it each day.
2. Begin to cultivate talking to God in prayer each day.
3. Go to a church that believes and teaches the Bible.
4. Share your decision with a close friend

If you have just received Jesus Christ into your life, we want to rejoice with you. Please send us an email at testimony@robinhealingministry.com.

Quotes

1. *Remember, except that fellowship touches us, we shall never have much power. . . . May God give us, today, such fellowship of His sufferings that when we see the person afflicted with any disease, we will pray right through until the roots of the disease are struck dead! When we see the lame and helpless man or woman, damaged, God, give us Your compassion, give us a fellowship with them, that shall undo their heavy burdens and set them free. How often we have missed the victory because we don't have the Lord's compassion at the needed moment. We failed to pray through with a broken heart.*

   — Smith Wigglesworth

2. *I know this, that the man or woman, who is to be possessed with zeal for God's work, can only possess it as he or she is hungry and thirsts after God.*

   —Smith Wigglesworth

3. *The Bible is the Word of God:*
      Supernatural in origin, eternal in duration
      Inexpressible in valor, infinite in scope
      Regenerative in power, infallible in authority

*Universal in interest, personal in application
Inspired in totality.
Read it through, write it down, pray it in, work it
out, and then pass it on.*
—Smith Wigglesworth

4. *Great faith is the product of great fights. Great testimonies are the outcome of great tests. Great triumphs come only out of great trials. Every stumbling block must become a stepping stone, and every opposition must become an opportunity.*
—Smith Wigglesworth

Notes

1. Barry Adams, Father Heart Communications, 1999–2008, www.FathersLoveLetter.com. Father love Letter used in page 77-83
2. Gene B. Moody, ordained minister, deliverance manual, 314–315. Prayers from deliverance used on page 43, 47, 53- 58
3. Robin Healing Ministry, Emmanuel Full Gospel Assemblies, Inc. website, plan of salvation, www. robinhealingministry.com. Plan of Salvation used from page plan of salvation page on website.
4. King James Version (KJV). Copyright © 1982 by Thomas Nelson, Inc
5. Amplified Bible (AMP), 1954, 1958, 1962, 1964, 1695, 1987, The Lockman Foundation.
6. Quotations: Smith Wigglesworth.
7. For more information on Father's Love Letter or the message of God's love, please visit www. FathersLoveLetter.com.
8. For more information on the plan of salvation and the message of hope, please visit www.robinhealingministry.com.

Miracles Still Happen

This book reveals practical keys and real-life examples for receiving miracles from God. It is not only mind-transforming, but it will also catapult your faith to another dimension in believing God for the impossible!

Miracles still happen! Are you looking for a miracle because of:

- An accumulation of trouble and stress in your life?
- Prayers that seemingly go unanswered?

- Questions that remain unanswered for long periods of time?
- Problems that remain unresolved?
- Broken marriages?
- Financial difficulties?
- Sickness and diseases in your body?

Then read *Miracles Still Happen* and discover answers and promises from God.

Every Day with Jesus
A Daily Encouragement and Prayer Journal

Every day with Jesus is indeed sweeter than the day before! You will be blessed by reading some encouraging Scriptures and writing in this daily encouragement and prayer journal.

Every Day with Jesus! This journal will help you spend time with Jesus every day. It will teach you:

- How to believe God for your miracle
- How to pray daily

- How to spend time with God
- How to wait upon God
- How to build a closer relationship with God

Another encouraging book by Robin Dinnanauth, this book is a daily devotional and prayer journal for those who are seeking a closer relationship with God.

Notes

Notes

Notes

Notes

Notes

Notes

Notes

Notes

Notes

Notes

Notes